THE BOOK
OF
THANKSGIVING

THE BOOK
OF
THANKSGIVING

STORIES, POEMS, AND
RECIPES FOR SHARING
ONE OF AMERICA'S
GREATEST HOLIDAYS

Jessica Faust AND *Jacky Sach*

CITADEL PRESS
Kensington Publishing Corp.
www.kensingtonbooks.com

CITADEL PRESS BOOKS are published by

Kensington Publishing Corp.
850 Third Avenue
New York, NY 10022

All Kensington titles, imprints, and distributed lines are available at special quantity discounts for bulk purchases for sales promotions, premiums, fund-raising, educational, or institutional use. Special book excerpts or customized printings can also be created to fit specific needs. For details, write or phone the office of the Kensington special sales manager: Kensington Publishing Corp., 850 Third Avenue, New York, NY 10022, attn: Special Sales Department, phone 1-800-221-2647.

First printing: September 2002

10 9 8 7 6 5 4 3 2 1

Printed in the United States of America

Text design by Stanley S. Drate / Folio Graphics Co. Inc.

Library of Congress Control Number: 2002104313

ISBN 0-8065-2367-0

To living with the spirit
of gratitude each and every day.

Contents

Acknowledgments

We would like to thank all of the people who have been so supportive of us throughout our endeavors—from kicking off BookEnds to writing this book and beyond . . .

We would both like to thank:

Bob Shuman, our editor at Citadel, for passing along this wonderful idea and giving us the chance to show we could pull it together.

Aimee Schnabel, Erica Rose, Amy Zavatto, Kris Curry, Jo-Anne Murphy, June Sach, Linda Faust, Rose Carroll, and Lila Faust, for contributing so many wonderful family recipes.

Jessica would like to thank:

Michael, for putting up with all my wacky creations.

Grandma Rose Carroll, for sharing with me all of her own recipes as well as those that have been in the family for years. But more importantly, for endowing me with a love of cooking.

Grandma Lila Faust, for always encouraging me in the kitchen, whether we were mixing up a batch of chocolate chip cookies or she was letting me loose so I could invent a ''secret recipe.''

Mom, for buying me my first Betty Crocker cookbook.

Dad and Christopher, for sitting through countless Betty Crocker meals.

Kris, Clare, Kim, and Jenny, for sharing a special Thanksgiving tradition that I hope will continue for years to come. And for allowing me to experiment with numerous vegetarian ''turkey'' recipes.

Jacky would like to thank:

Mom, for all the pastry lessons, the laughter, and the wonderful advice.

And the guys in my life who have made holidays so fun: my husband, Alex, my stepson, Alex, my brothers, Pete and Dave, and the wonderful memories of Dad.

1

A Thanksgiving Tale

The unthankful heart . . . discovers no mercies;
but let the thankful heart sweep through the day and,
as the magnet finds the iron, so it will find,
in every hour, some heavenly blessings!

—Henry Ward Beecher

Thanksgiving is a holiday with a rich past, and while many of us know that it began with the Pilgrims and Native American Indians, few know the true beginnings of Thanksgiving. Here, in just a few short pages, you'll learn about the Separatists and the Strangers, a Brave named Samoset, and a place called Plymouth Rock.

Here is the story of Thanksgiving from the first feast to the first official presidential proclamation. This is a story that every family should share on Thanksgiving to remind themselves of all that they truly have to give thanks for.

*T*hanksgiving as we know it today usually consists of turkey, stuffing, the Macy's Thanksgiving Day Parade, football, and plenty of naps. It is a time to gather with family and friends, and of course, it is the day before the biggest shopping day of the year and the beginning of the holiday season.

Hundreds of years ago, though, the first Thanksgiving had quite a different meaning, a meaning that often gets lost in today's hurried culture. So why was the first Thanksgiving celebrated? We all know about the Pilgrims and Indians, but who were these people who started our country and one of our country's greatest holidays?

Before looking at the actual day of Thanksgiving, we must first look at the people behind it, the Pilgrims. The word "pilgrim" literally means a person who journeys to a sacred place or a traveler, and that's exactly what the Pilgrims were doing.

Many of the Pilgrims were English Puritans who felt the Church of England never completed the work of the Reformation. Because of this, they broke from the Church to commit themselves to a life based on the Bible. Most of these Separatists were farmers, poorly educated and without social or political standing.

In 1609, long before the Pilgrims were Pilgrims, a group of English Separatists fled their native England and the religious persecution they were facing to begin life in a place where they had freedom and security. Traveling to Holland, they not only found the freedoms they were seeking, but enjoyed a very prosperous life. However, eleven short years later, these Separatists had begun to feel that Holland was not providing them with the life they wanted to live. Not only were they unable to gain the economic freedoms they had hoped for, but many of the Separatists began to worry that their children were becoming too entrenched in the Dutch way of life, one they considered frivolous.

Once again in search of a new home, the Separatists, or Pilgrims as they were soon to be called, decided to travel to the

New World, what we know today as America or the United States of America. In order to pay for the notoriously expensive trip to traveling to the New World, the Pilgrims negotiated an agreement with Thomas Weston, a London iron merchant. The agreement was originally between the Pilgrims, in their search for religious freedom and the London Merchants represented by Thomas Weston. Unfortunately however, the Pilgrims found the arrangements too restrictive and were never able to come to terms with Weston. Without an agreement that would assist the Pilgrims in their new life, the group set out on a small ship called the *Speedwell*, but were forced to turn back when she proved to be unseaworthy. Upon returning to port, the passengers and cargo were loaded on to the *Mayflower*.

Aboard the *Mayflower*

On September 16, 1620, the Separatists boarded a ship called the *Mayflower* to begin their historic voyage across the Atlantic. Carrying one hundred and two passengers, thirty-seven of whom were considered Separatists, the ship traveled for sixty-five days. However luxurious the *Mayflower* may have been, life aboard the vessel was anything but easy. For fear of fire, the passengers and crew were required to eat all their food cold or uncooked and the trip was damp and cold. Two passengers died during the crossing: a young boy named William Butten, a servant-apprentice to Dr. Samuel Fuller, and a *Mayflower* crew member whose name is not known. One woman, Elizabeth Hopkins, gave birth while at sea, to a son she named Oceanus.

On November 19, the passengers of one of this country's most renowned sailing ships finally saw land. When the crew

---

Mayflower was a very common ship name, and in fact many other ships named *Mayflower* made trips to New England; but none of them was the same ship that brought the Pilgrims to America.

Mayflower Passenger List

John Alden
Issac Allerton
Mary Allerton (wife)
Bartholomew Allerton (son)
Mary Allerton (daughter)
Remember Allerton (daughter)
Don Allerton (no relation to other
  Allertons)
Don Billington
Eleanor Billington (wife)
Frances Billington (relation unkown)
John Billington (son)
William Bradford
Dorothy May Bradford (wife)
William Brewster
Mary Brewster (wife)
Love Brewster (son)
Wrestling Brewster (son)
Richard Britteridge
Peter Brown
William Butten
Robert Cartier
John Carver
Katherine Carver (wife)
James Chilton
Susanna Chilton (wife)
Mary Chilton (unknown relation)
Richard Clarke
Francis Cooke
John Cooke (son)
Humility Cooper
John Crackston
John Crackston (son)
Edward Doty
Francis Eaton
Sarah Eaton (wife)
Samuel Eaton (son)
(first name unknown) Ely (sailor)

Thomas English
Moses Fletcher
Edward Fuller
Ann Fuller (wife)
Samuel Fuller (son)
Samuel Fuller (not related,
  physician)
Richard Gardiner
John Goodman
William Holbeck
John Hooke
Steven Hopkins
Elizabeth Hopkins (wife)
Giles Hopkins (son)
Constance Hopkins (daughter)
Damaris Hopkins (daughter)
Oceanis Hopkins (son, born during
  voyage)
John Howland
John Langmore
William Latham
Edward Leister
Edmund Margeson
Christopher Martin
Marie Martin
Desire Minter
Elinor More
Jasper More
Richard More
Mary More
William Mullins
Alice Mullins (wife)
Joseph Mullins (son)
Priscilla Mullins (daughter)
Degory Priest
Solomon Prower
John Rigdale
Alice Rigdale

Thomas Rogers
Joseph Rogers (son)
Henry Sampson
George Soule
Miles Standish
Rose Standish (wife)
Elias Story
Edward Thompson
Edward Tilley
Agnes Tilley (wife)
John Tilley
Joan Tilley (wife)
Elizabeth Tilley (John's daughter)
Thomas Tinker
(The wife of Thomas Tinker, name
    unknown)
(The son of Thomas Tinker, name
    unknown)
William Trevore
John Turner
(Two sons of John Turner,
    unknown)
Master Richard Warren
William White
Susana White (wife)
Peregrine White (son)
Resolved White (son)
Roger Wilder
Thomas Williams
Edward Winslow
Elizabeth Winslow (wife)
Gilbert Winslow (brother)

of the *Mayflower* first spotted Cape Cod, they immediately directed the ship south, toward Virginia and the land Sir Edwin Sandys, treasurer of the London Company, had granted them. Two days later, however, on November 21, the ship turned around and anchor was dropped in what is now Provincetown, Massachusetts.

Life on Land

As one can imagine, one hundred and two people living together aboard a ship led to many disagreements between the Separatists, who liked to call themselves the "Saints," and the crew and other passengers, whom the Separatists referred to as "Strangers." After the ship landed in Massachusetts, a meeting was held and an agreement, the *Mayflower* Compact, was worked out. The agreement, which created the colony's own government, guaranteed equality and unified the two groups. Together they named themselves "Pilgrims."

It wasn't until December 21 that the Pilgrims finally settled in Plymouth Harbor or landed on Plymouth Rock. Plymouth offered both an excellent harbor and a large brook with a great

The Mayflower Compact read as follows: *"In the name of God, Amen. We, whose names are underwritten, the Loyal Subjects of our dread Sovereign Lord, King James, by the Grace of God, of England, France and Ireland, King, Defender of the Faith. Having undertaken for the Glory of God, and Advancement of the Christian Faith, and the Honour of our King and Country, a voyage to plant the first colony in the northern parts of Virginia; do by these presents, solemnly and mutually in the Presence of God and one of another, covenant and combine ourselves together into a civil body Politick, for our better Ordering and Preservation, and Furtherance of the Ends aforesaid; And by Virtue hereof to enact, constitute, and frame, such just and equal Laws, Ordinances, Acts, Constitutions and Offices, from time to time, as shall be thought most meet and convenient for the General good of the Colony; unto which we promise all due submission and obedience. In Witness whereof we have hereunto subscribed our names at Cape Cod the eleventh of November, in the Reign of our Sovereign Lord, King James of England, France and Ireland, the eighteenth, and of Scotland the fifty-fourth. Anno Domini, 1620."*

supply of fish. At this point, the biggest concern the Pilgrims had was their fear of the local Native American Indians. It wasn't long, however, before their neighbors proved themselves to be peaceful.

The first winter in Plymouth was devastating for the Pilgrims. Because they had waited so late in the year to finally settle their colony, the cold, snow, and sleet did nothing but interfere with the work they were trying to do. Unfortunately, the brutal weather took its toll and many died during the long winter. Of the one hundred and two Pilgrims and crew who left England in September, only fifty were left living when warmer weather arrived in March.

One of the most important events in Pilgrim history took place on March 16, 1621. On this date, an Indian brave, Samoset of the Wampanoag tribe, walked into the Plymouth settlement and called out in English, "Welcome."

What Is Plymouth Rock?

Plymouth Rock is a granite boulder in Pilgrim Memorial State Park in Plymouth, Massachusetts, with the date 1620 carved on it. According to legend, it's the spot where Pilgrim explorers stepped off the *Mayflower* when they landed on December 21, 1620. While many historians doubt that the Pilgrims actually stepped on the rock, it serves as a memorial to the landing of the Pilgrims.

The Wampanoag Indians were part of the Woodland Culture area of Indians and lived along what is now the coast of Massachusetts and Rhode Island. This group of people did not live in tipis like the Indians of the Great Plains, but instead lived in round-roofed houses called wigwams.

The Wampanoags were a traveling tribe and moved several times during the year in search of food. In the spring Wampanoags would fish the rivers for salmon and herring. During planting season they moved to the forest to hunt deer and other animals, and after hunting season, they moved inland, where there was greater protection from the weather and they could live on food they had stored during the earlier months.

Samoset had originally been from the Wabanake tribe but was living with the Wampanoags because of his friendship with Squanto. Both men had left their native homes with English explorers and eventually met in England, where they learned to speak English.

Squanto was originally from the village of Patuxet and a member of the Pokanokit Wampanoag nation. Patuxet had once stood on the exact site where the Pilgrims built Plymouth. When Squanto and Samoset returned home in 1620, the village was deserted and skeletons were everywhere. Everyone in the village had died from an illness the English slavers had left behind. Squanto and Samoset went to stay in the neighboring Wampanoag village.

In the spring of the following year, Squanto and Samoset

Native American Cultures

When the Europeans or white settlers first landed on the North American continent not only did they meet a new culture of people—the Native Americans—but they quickly learned that not all Native Americans were alike. While most people know that Native Americans come from many different tribes, few are aware of the cultural groups these tribes come from. Just like the United States has many different States with individual customs, we also have different cultures made up of separate groupings of states, best described as the Midwest, South, Southwest, Northeast, etc. Each area of the country has different customs and different accents, just as individual Native American cultural groups had their own languages and customs.

Native American cultural groups are best categorized by the areas in which the tribes lived. Each had its own way of finding food and building houses depending on the natural resources that were best available to them. For example, the Plains Indians, located in what we now call North Dakota on south to Texas, lived in tepees, ate buffalo, and wore buffalo skin clothing, while the Woodland Indians usually lived in longhouses or wigwams and ate deer, rabbit, squirrel, and berries. In fact, the modern-day game of lacrosse was invented by the Woodland Indians.

were hunting along the beach and were startled to see people from England in their deserted village. Finally, after several days, they decided to approach them.

Because of the kindness of these men, it wasn't long before a kinship developed. From Squanto, the Pilgrims learned how to tap the maple trees for sap, how to plant corn, and which plants were poisonous and which had medicinal powers. He also taught them how to build Indian-style houses, and even dig and cook clams.

Thanks to the help of the Indians, the Pilgrims were able to enjoy a plentiful harvest come October. Not only were they healthy and alive, but now they had enough corn, fruits, vegetables, fish, and meat to store away for winter.

Just one year after their arrival in the New World, the Pilgrims had much to celebrate. They had built homes, raised crops, and even made friends with their Indian neighbors. They had beaten the odds and it was time to celebrate.

In honor of all they had done, Pilgrim Governor William Bradford proclaimed a day of thanksgiving to be shared by all the colonists and the neighboring Indians. Together the fifty Pilgrims and ninety Indians shared a celebration feast that lasted three days. They played games and showed off their various skills. The Indians demonstrated the powers of the bow and arrow, while the Pilgrims showed off their muskets.

The Indians planted corn by heaping the earth into low mounds with several seeds and fish in each mound. The decaying fish fertilzed the corn and produced bountiful crops.

Unfortunately, the following year wasn't as bountiful. More and more Separatists were making the trip to the New World. The larger number of people and the Pilgrims' inability to fully master the art of growing corn and other vegetables put a horrible strain on supplies and food stores.

The real beginning of present-day Thanksgiving, it is believed, was during the Pilgrims' third year in the New World. The spring and summer of 1623 were hot and dry, leaving the crops dying in the fields. Knowing how much the Pilgrims needed a successful planting season, Governor Bradford ordered a day of fasting and prayer. It wasn't much later that the rains came and the crops were saved. To celebrate, it was proclaimed that November 29 of that year was a day of thanksgiving. Modern-day thanksgiving is still celebrated in late November.

The early Thanksgiving celebrations were filled with joy and gratitude for the rain and bounty of food. A feast was eaten outside and included venison provided by the Indians and enough wild fowl to supply the village for a week. The fowl would have included ducks, geese, turkeys, and even swans. Other items served at the feast probably included clams and other shellfish, smoked eel, groundnuts (a kind of potato-like root) baked in hot ashes, peas, salad greens, herbs, corn pone, and a corn-rye bread brought by the Indians. The Pilgrims also served wine made from wild grapes.

Thanksgivings for Years to Come

While celebrating an annual thanksgiving continued through the years, a day of national thanksgiving wasn't even suggested until during the American Revolution. In 1777, General George Washington and his army were instructed by the Continental Congress to stop in the open fields on their way to Valley Forge, despite the bitter weather, to mark Thanksgiving.

As the nation's first president, George Washington's first presidential proclamation after his inauguration in 1789 declared November 26, 1789, as a national day of "thanksgiving and prayer."

President Washington's Thanksgiving Day Proclamation—1778

Whereas it is the duty of all nations to acknowledge the providence of Almighty God, to obey His will, to be grateful for His benefits, and humbly to implore His protection and favor; and Whereas both Houses of Congress have, by their joint committee, requested me "to recommend to the people of the United States a day of public thanksgiving and prayer, to be observed by acknowledging with grateful hearts the many and signal favors of Almighty God, especially by affording them an opportunity peaceably to establish a form of government for their safety and happiness:"

Now, therefore, I do recommend and assign Thursday, the 26th day of November next, to be devoted by the people of these States to the service of that great and glorious Being who is the beneficent author of all the good that was, that is, or that will be; that we may then all unite in rendering unto Him our sincere and humble thanks for His kind care and protection of the people of this country previous to their becoming a nation; for the signal and manifold mercies and the favorable interpositions of His providence in the course and conclusion of the late war; for the great degree of tranquility, union, and plenty which we have since enjoyed; for the peaceable and rational manner in which we have been enable to establish constitutions of government for our safety and happiness, and particularly the national one now lately instituted for the civil and religious liberty with which we are blessed, and the means we have of acquiring and diffusing useful knowledge; and, in general, for all the great and various favors which He has been pleased to confer upon us.

And also that we may then unite in most humbly offering our prayers and supplications to the great Lord and Ruler of Nations and beseech Him to pardon our national and other transgressions; to enable us all, whether in public or private stations, to perform our several and relative duties properly and punctually; to render our National Government a blessing to all the people by constantly being a Government of wise, just, and constitutional laws, discreetly and faithfully executed and obeyed; to protect and guide all sovereigns and nations (especially such as have shown kindness to us), and to bless them with good governments, peace, and concord; to promote the knowledge and practice of true religion and virtue, and the increase of science among them and us; and, generally to grant unto all mankind such a degree of temporal prosperity as He alone knows to be best.

Given under my hand, at the city of New York, the 3d day of October, AD 1789.

[signed] G. Washington

In the early 1800s, the presidential thanksgiving proclamations ceased for about forty-five years. Except for New York State, which adopted Thanksgiving Day as an annual custom in 1817, no official mention was made of the holiday. By the middle of the nineteenth century, many states, including Connecticut, Maine, Vermont, Iowa, Pennsylvania, and Missouri, were celebrating Thanksgiving Day, but it wasn't until 1863 when President Lincoln declared a national Thanksgiving holiday that Thanksgiving as we know it today became a tradition.

On October 3, 1863, President Lincoln declared the last Thursday in November to be set aside as a national day of Thanksgiving. This became the first in the unbroken series of holidays that we still celebrate today.

President Lincoln's First Thanksgiving Day Proclamation—October 3, 1863

The year that is drawing towards its close, has been filled with the blessings of fruitful fields and healthful skies. To these bounties, which are so constantly enjoyed that we are prone to forget the source from which they come, others have been added, which are of so extraordinary a nature, that they cannot fail to penetrate and soften even the heart which is habitually insensible to the ever watchful providence of Almighty God. In the midst of a civil war of unequalled magnitude and severity, which has sometimes seemed to foreign States to invite and to provoke their aggression, peace has been preserved with all nations, order has been maintained, the laws have been respected and obeyed, and harmony has prevailed everywhere except in the theatre of military conflict; while that theatre has been greatly contracted by the advancing armies and navies of the Union. Needful diversions of wealth and of strength from the fields of peaceful industry to the national defence, have not arrested the plough, the shuttle, or the ship; the axe had enlarged the borders of our settlements, and the mines, as well of iron and coal as of the precious metals, have yielded even more abundantly than heretofore. Population has steadily increased, notwithstanding the waste that has been made in the camp, the siege and the battlefield; and the country, rejoicing in the consciousness of augmented strength and vigor, is permitted to expect continuance of years with large increase of freedom.

No human counsel hath devised nor hath any mortal hand

worked out these great things. They are the gracious gifts of the Most High God, who, while dealing with us in anger for our sins, hath nevertheless remembered mercy. It has seemed to me fit and proper that they should be solemnly, reverently and gratefully acknowledged as with one heart and voice by the whole American People. I do therefore invite my fellow citizens in every part of the United States, and also those who are at sea and those who are sojourning in foreign lands, to set apart and observe the last Thursday of November next, as a day of Thanksgiving and Praise to our beneficent Father who dwelleth in the Heavens. And I recommend to them that while offering up the ascriptions justly due to Him for such singular deliverances and blessings, they do also, with humble penitence for our national perverseness and disobedience, commend to his tender care all those who have become widows, orphans, mourners or sufferers in the lamentable civil strife in which we are unavoidably engaged, and fervently implore the interposition of the Almighty Hand to heal the wounds of the nation and to restore it as soon as may be consistent with the Divine purposes to the full enjoyment of peace, harmony, tranquillity and Union.

—Abraham Lincoln

In 1939, the country was still struggling to recover from the Great Depression. In order to help, President Franklin D. Roosevelt moved Thanksgiving from the fourth Thursday in November to the third Thursday. His hope was that adding one extra week to Christmas shopping would give the economy a boost.

Unfortunately, while many states picked up on the change, others continued to celebrate on the last Thursday of the month. In 1941, Congress solved the problem by decreeing that Thanksgiving should fall on the fourth Thursday of November, and to this day the proclamation still stands.

2

Prayers and Poems of Thanksgiving

Not what we say about our blessings,
but how we use them,
is the true measure of our thanksgiving.

—W. T. Purkiser

The Pilgrims and Native Americans were both very religious people, and their first Thanksgiving was a way to give thanks for all that God and nature had given to them that year. So, in the spirit of the Pilgrims and the Native Americans, this year when you sit down to your Thanksgiving meal, take the time to think of all the things you are thankful for, from the food on the table to the people around it.

Whether you have a special or traditional grace you usually say, or if you would like to try something new, these prayers, songs, and poems—including some Native American blessings—will make terrific opening blessings for your meal.

Psalm 100

Make a joyful noise unto the
Lord, all the lands!
Serve the Lord with gladness!
Come into His presence with singing!
Know that the Lord is God!
It is He that made us, and we are His;
we are His people,
and the sheep of His pasture.
Enter His gates with thanksgiving
and His courts with praise!
Give thanks to Him, bless His name!
For the Lord is good;
His steadfast love endures for ever,
and His faithfulness to all generations.

Psalm 111

Full of honor and majesty in His work,
and His righteousness endures for ever.
He has caused His wonderful works to be remembered;
the Lord is gracious and merciful
He provides food for those who fear Him;
he is ever mindful of His covenant.
He has shown His people the power of His works,
in giving them the heritage of the nations.
The works of His hands are faithful and just;
all of His precepts are trustworthy,
they are established for ever and ever,
to be performed with faithfulness and uprightness.
He sent redemption to His people;
he has commanded His covenant for ever.
Holy and terrible is His name!
The fear of the Lord is the beginning of wisdom;
a good understanding have all those who practice it,
His praise endures for ever!

Psalm 145:15–16

The eyes of all look to you, Lord.
You give us our food when we need it.
You open your hand and satisfy the desires of every living
thing.

Aztec Prayer

Lord most giving and resourceful,
I implore you;
make it your will
that this people enjoy
the goods and riches you naturally give,
that naturally issue from you,
that are pleasing and savory,
that delight and comfort,
though lasting but briefly,
passing away as if in a dream.

A Hebrew Blessing ✳

Blessed are You, O Lord our God, Eternal King,
Who feeds the whole world with Your goodness,
With grace, with loving kindness, and with tender mercy.
You give food to all flesh,
For Your loving kindness endures forever.
Through Your great goodness, food has never failed us.
O may it not fail us forever, for Your name's sake,
Since You nourish and sustain all living things,
And do good to all,
And provide food for all Your creatures
Whom You have created.
Blessed are You, O Lord, Who gives food to all.

A Prayer From Mohammad (570–632)

O Lord, grant us to love Thee;
Grant that we may love those that love Thee;
Grant that we may do the deeds that win Thy love.
Make the love of Thee be dearer to us than ourselves, than our
families, than wealth, and even than cool water.

The Prayer of St. Francis of Assissi

Lord, make me an instrument of Your peace.
Where there is hatred, let me sow love;
Where there is injury, pardon;
Where there is doubt, faith;
Where there is despair, hope;
Where there is darkness, light; and
Where there is sadness, joy.
O Divine Master, grant that I may not so much seek to be
consoled,
as to console;
To be understood, as to understand;
To be loved, as to love.
For it is in giving that we receive—
It is in pardoning that we are pardoned;
And it is in dying that we are born to eternal life.

Iroquois Prayer

We return thanks to Our Mother, The Earth, which sustains us. We return thanks to the rivers and streams, which supply us with water. We return thanks to all herbs, which furnish medicines for the cure of our diseases. We return thanks to the corn, and to her sisters, the beans and squash, which give us life. We return thanks to the bushes and trees, which provide us with fruit. We return thanks to the wind, which, moving the air, has banished diseases. We return thanks to the moon and the stars, which have given us their light when the sun was gone. We return thanks to Our Grandfather He-no, that He has protected His grandchildren from witches and reptiles, and has given to us His rain. We return thanks to the sun, that he has looked upon the earth with a beneficent eye. Lastly, we return thanks to the Great Spirit, in Whom is embodied all goodness, and Who directs all things for the good of His children.

Blessings and Poems

Praise to God who giveth meat
Convenient unto all who eat
Praise for tea and buttered toast
Father, Son, and Holy Ghost.

—*Scottish Grace*

ᔑᓎᔡ

Father of all—God!
What we have here is of Thee;
Take our thanks and bless us,
That we may continue to do Thy will.

—*Lew Wallace*

ᔑᓎᔡ

Father we thank Thee for this food,
for health and strength and all things good.
May others all these blessings share,
and hearts be grateful everywhere.

ᔑᓎᔡ

Some hae meat and canna eat,
And some wad eat that want it;
But we hae meat and we can eat,
And sae the Lord be thanit.

—*Robert Burns*

ᔑᓎᔡ

For each new morning with its light,
For rest and shelter of the night,
For health and food, for love and friends,
For everything Thy goodness sends.

—*Ralph Waldo Emerson*

ᔑᓎᔡ

Though our mouths were full of song as the sea,
and our tongues of exultation as the multitude of its waves,
and our lips of praise as the wide-extended firmament;
though our eyes shone with light like the sun and the moon,
and our hands were spread forth like the eagles of heaven,
and our feet were swift as hinds,
we should still be unable to thank Thee and bless Thy name,
O Lord our God and God of our fathers,
for one thousandth or one ten thousandth part
of the bounties which Thou has bestowed
upon our fathers and upon us.

—*The Hebrew Prayer Book*

∞

Our Father in Heaven,
We give thanks for the pleasure
of gathering together for this occasion.
We give thanks for this food
prepared by loving hands.
We give thanks for life, the freedom
to enjoy it all and all other blessings.
As we partake of this food,
We pray for health and strength to carry on
and try to live as You would have us.
This we ask in the name of Christ
Our Heavenly Father.

—*Harry Jewell*

∞

Bless us O Lord, for these gifts, we are about
to receive from your bounty.

∞

Be present at our table, Lord;
be here, and everywhere adored;
Thy mercies bless and grant that we
may feast in fellowship with Thee. Amen.

∞

Thank you, Lord, for each new day You give to me,
For earth and sky and sand and sea,
For rainbows after springtime showers,
Autumn leaves and summer flowers,
Winter snowscapes so serene,
Harvest fields of gold and green,
Beauty shining all around,
Lilac scent and robin sound,
Stars that twinkle high above
And all the people that I love.

—Anonymous

❧

The Lord is good to me
and so I thank the Lord
For giving me
the things I need
The sun and the rain
and the appleseed
The Lord is good to me.

❧

God is great, God is good
Let us thank Him for our food
By His hands we all are fed
Give us Lord our daily bread
Amen.

❧

Bless us, oh Lord,
for these thy gifts,
which we are about to receive,
from thy bounty, through Christ our Lord.
Amen.

The Pilgrims Came
(Author Unknown)

The Pilgrims came across the sea,
And never thought of you and me;
And yet it's very strange the way
We think of them Thanksgiving day.

We tell their story, old and true
Of how they sailed across the blue,
And found a new land to be free
And built their homes quite near the sea.

Every child knows well the tale
Of how they bravely turned the sail
And journeyed many a day and night,
To worship God as they thought right.

Giving Thanks
(Author Unknown)

For the hay and the corn and the wheat that is reaped,
For the labor well done, and the barns that are heaped,
For the sun and the dew and the sweet honeycomb,
For the rose and the song and the harvest brought home—
Thanksgiving! Thanksgiving!

For the trade and the skill and the wealth in our land,
For the cunning and strength of the workingman's hand,
For the good that our artists and poets have taught,
For the friendship that hope and affection have brought—
Thanksgiving! Thanksgiving!

For the homes that with purest affection are blest,
For the season of plenty and well-deserved rest,
For our country extending from sea unto sea;
The land that is known as the "Land of the Free"—
Thanksgiving! Thanksgiving!

Songs

Over the River

Over the river and through the wood
To Grandfather's house we go.
  The horse knows the way
  To carry the sleigh
Through white and drifted snow.

Over the river and through the wood—
Oh, how the wind does blow!
  It stings the toes
  And bites the nose,
As over the ground we go.

Over the river and through the wood
To have a first-rate play.
  Hear the bells ring,
  Ting-a-ling-ling!
Hurrah for Thanksgiving Day!

Over the river and through the wood,
Trot fast, my dapple gray!
  Spring over the ground
  Like a hunting hound,
For this is Thanksgiving Day.

Over the river and through the wood,
And straight through the barnyard gate.
  We seem to go
  Extremely slow—
It is so hard to wait!

Over the river and through the wood—
Now Grandmother's cap I spy!
  Hurrah for fun!
  Is the pudding done?
Hurrah for the pumpkin pie!

All Things Bright and Beautiful

Refrain
All things bright and beautiful,
All creatures great and small,
All things wise and wonderful:
The Lord God made them all.

Each little flower that opens,
Each little bird that sings,
God made their glowing colors,
And made their tiny wings.
(Refrain)

The purple-headed mountains,
The river running by,
The sunset and the morning
That brightens up the sky.
(Refrain)

The cold wind in the winter,
The pleasant summer sun,
The ripe fruits in the garden:
God made them every one.
(Refrain)

God gave us eyes to see them,
And lips that we might tell
How great is God Almighty,
Who has made all things well.
(Refrain)

We Gather Together

We gather together to ask the Lord's blessing;
He chastens and hastens His will to make known;
The wicked oppressing now cease from distressing,
Sing praises to his name: He forgets not His own.

Beside us to guide us, our God with us joining,
Ordaining, maintaining His kingdom divine;
So from the beginning the fight we were winning;
Thou, Lord, wast at our side, All glory be Thine!

We all do extol Thee, Thou leader triumphant,
And pray that Thou still our defender wilt be.
Let Thy congregation escape tribulation;
Thy name be ever praised! O Lord, make us free!
Amen

Family Favorites

Everyone has prayers and blessings that are traditionally used on Thanksgiving. Write down your family favorites here.

TITLE _____

_____

_____

_____

_____

_____

_____

_____

_____

_____

_____

_____

❧❧

TITLE _____

_____

_____

_____

_____

_____

_____

_____

_____

_____

_____

_____

_____

TITLE _____

_____

_____

_____

_____

_____

_____

_____

_____

_____

_____

_____

_____

_____

❖❖

TITLE _____

_____

_____

_____

_____

_____

_____

_____

_____

_____

_____

_____

_____

_____

TITLE _____

_____

_____

_____

_____

_____

_____

_____

_____

_____

_____

_____

_____

_____

_____

3

Cooking Up Thanks

An optimist is a person who starts a new diet on Thanksgiving Day.
—Irv Kupcinet

While the meal is important at any event or for any holiday, there is nothing quite like Thanksgiving, when the entire holiday is essentially centered around what you are going to eat. Because of that, not only do we have a number of different recipes to offer, but we have everything ranging from soup to nuts (literally). You'll find old family favorites from our families, as well as space to add those favorites that your family has been enjoying for years.

When sitting down to plan your Thanksgiving dinner, it is important to remember one thing—we are here to give thanks for the abundance we have, not necessarily to cook in abundance. So pick those few things your family most enjoys and toss the rest. No one needs to take home the four pounds of leftover stuffing that you made simply because Grandma always did.

Here are some of our favorite Thanksgiving foods.

APPETIZERS

These tasty treats can be set on the table beforehand for early-arriving guests or served right at the table as a prequel to the delicious meal ahead. Either way, you'll discover that they add a bit of pizzazz to what is often a predictable meal.

Harvest Appetizer

This easy appetizer is the perfect treat while waiting for the turkey to arrive. From the recipe files of Linda Faust.

> 1 large eggplant
> 1/4 cup grated onion
> 1 cup fine chopped tomatoes
> 1 1/2 tbsp chopped parsley
> 1/4 cup olive oil
> 1 1/2 tbsp vinegar (red wine or balsamic)
> salt and pepper to taste
> 2 packages pita bread

Preheat oven to 400 degrees F.

Wash eggplant, and place on a lightly greased jelly roll pan or cookie sheet. Bake for 50 minutes.

When finished baking, dip eggplant in cold water, then hold by stem and remove skin. Discard stem and skin.

Chop eggplant, and add onion, tomato, and parsley. Then add oil, vinegar, and salt and pepper. Chill.

Cut pita with scissors into triangles. Spread eggplant mixture on pita triangles or use as a dip.

Baked Fruit Compote

From the files of Erica Rose, this terrific start to your meal is different from the traditional green salad and sure to make you a star.

³/₄ cup fresh orange juice

¹/₄ cup maple syrup

¹/₄ cup sugar

¹/₂ lemon, sliced thin with the seeds removed

¹/₈ tsp salt

1 cinnamon stick

4 whole cloves

¹/₄ cup plus 1 tbsp fresh lemon juice, divided

3 large baking apples, pared and sliced into ¹/₂-inch slices

2 large baking pears, quartered and cored

2 bananas, sliced crosswise and then cut into chunks

³/₄ cup seeded, halved dark grapes

Preheat oven to 350 degrees F.

In a saucepan, place the orange juice, maple syrup, sugar, lemon slices, cinnamon stick, cloves, and salt. Bring to a boil, stirring. Then remove from heat and set aside.

Add ¹/₄ cup lemon juice to a shallow 2¹/₂-quart baking dish. Add apples and pears, and mix well. The lemon juice will prevent the fruits from turning brown.

Pour orange juice mixture over the fruit, cover loosely, and bake for 20 minutes.

While the fruit is baking, peel the bananas and slice in half crosswise, then lengthwise. Sprinkle with remaining tablespoon of lemon juice; add to baking dish with grapes, gently mixing them with the cooking syrup.

Cover loosely and bake for 10 minutes more or until the fruit is just fork tender. May be served warm or cold.

Deviled Eggs

No Faust-Goze Thanksgiving is complete without Nick's famous deviled eggs!

MAKES 8 EGGS.

> 8 eggs
> 1/2 tsp prepared mustard
> 1 tbsp mayonnaise
> salt and pepper to taste
> 1 pinch paprika

Place the eggs in a saucepan and cover with water. Bring to a boil. Cover, remove from heat, and let eggs sit in hot water for 10 to 12 minutes. Remove from hot water and cool.

Peel eggs and cut each egg in half lengthwise. Remove yolks and place them in a small bowl. When all the eggs have been peeled, combine mustard, mayonnaise, and salt and pepper with yolks. Mix until smooth.

Refill each egg half with the yolk mixture and sprinkle with paprika.

Roasted Pumpkin Seeds

An especially perfect treat for an autumn holiday. These great starters are a fun way to get the kids involved in cooking.

MAKES 1 1/2 CUPS.

> 1 1/2 cups raw whole pumpkin seeds
> 2 tsp butter, melted
> 1 pinch garlic salt

Preheat oven to 300 degrees F.

Toss seeds together with the melted butter and garlic. Spread the seeds in a single layer on a baking sheet and bake for about 45 minutes or until golden brown; stir occasionally.

CRUDITE AND A CHOICE OF DIPS

The perfect beginning to any meal is a platter full of assorted fruits and vegetables. The light an healthy snacks will tide over your "starved" guests and get your Thanksgiving party started on the right foot.

The following vegetable dips are delicious with carrots, celery, broccoli, cucumbers, cauliflower, cherry tomatoes, green onions or scallions, red, green or yellow peppers, zucchini, or radishes. Whatever you choose, give your guests a choice of two or three of these delicious dips.

Cucumber Dip

1 cup creamed, fine curd cottage cheese

1/2 medium cucumber, grated (about 1/4 cup)

1/2 tsp seasoned salt

1/4 tsp Worcestershire sauce

2 tbsp lemon juice

Combine all ingredients, mix well and chill.

Dill Dip

1 cup sour cream

1 cup mayonnaise

1 tsp dried dill

1 tsp dried chives

1 tsp parsley flakes

3 shakes Worcestershire sauce

Combine all ingredients and mix well.

Garden Dip

❖❖

1 (8-ounce) package cream cheese, softened
1 can Campbell's condensed tomato soup
2 tbsp finely chopped celery
2 tbsp thinly sliced green onions
2 tbsp finely chopped parsley
2 tbsp horseradish
Dashes of garlic powder, salt, pepper and hot pepper sauce

Mix all ingredients together and let chill for 2 hours or overnight.

Fruit Dip

❖❖

This is delicious served with apples, oranges, berries, pineapple, pears, or whatever your favorites are.

1 cup mayonnaise
1 cup marshmallow crème
1 tsp ginger
1 grated orange peel

Mix, chill, serve, and enjoy.

SOUPS AND SALADS

Any meal seems more special if started out right, with a cool crisp salad or warm bowl of soup. What you choose to start your Thanksgiving feast with is really up to you. The most exciting thing about some of these recipes is that they are not only a delicious addition to your meal, but a terrific centerpiece for your table.

Soup in a Pumpkin

❧❧

This delightful recipe not only is delicious, but makes a great centerpiece or decoration to your table. From the recipe box of Linda Faust.

SERVES 8 TO 10 PEOPLE.

> 2¹/₂ cups fresh crumbs from homemade-type white bread, crust off, lightly pressed down
> 4 ounces (1 stick) butter, plus 2 tbsp or so soft butter
> 2 cups minced onions
> 1 6- to 7-pound healthy, unblemished pumpkin
> 2 to 2¹/₂ quarts chicken stock, brought to simmer
> 1¹/₂ cups coarsely grated Swiss cheese
> Seasonings: salt, freshly ground pepper, ¹/₂ tsp sage
> 1 cup heavy cream
> ¹/₂ cup and chopped fresh parsley, lightly pressed down

Spread crumbs in a roasting pan and dry them out in a 350-degree F oven for 15 minutes, once or twice tossing them about—they should hardly color.

Meanwhile, melt stick of butter and slowly cook the minced onions in it until the onions are perfectly tender and translucent—about 15 minutes.

Toss the crumbs into the onions and cook, stirring, for 3 minutes.

PREPARING PUMPKIN:
Preheat oven to 400 degrees F.

Cut a neat cover out of the pumpkin, scrape out the seeds and strings, and rub the inner flesh of the pumpkin and the cover with remaining 2 tbsp soft butter. Set the pumpkin on a lightly buttered baking sheet.

Heat chicken stock to a slow simmer.

Turn the crumb mixture into the pumpkin, stir in the grated cheese, and fill the pumpkin to within 2 inches of its top with hot chicken stock. Season to taste with salt, pepper, and sage. Set the pumpkin at once in the lower level of the oven. Bake until the pumpkin has just softened (about 90 minutes)—but do not overcook, or it will collapse!!!

NOTE: You may keep the pumpkin soup warm for 30 minutes in a 175-degree F oven until ready to serve—too much heat and too long a wait will dangerously soften the pumpkin and then oops—collapse!!!

TO SERVE: Just before serving, bring the cream almost to simmer; gently stir it into the soup, followed by the chopped parsley. At the table, ladle the soup into hot bowls, scraping off some of the flesh from inside the pumpkin as you do so.

HEY! For a nice side to your pumpkin soup, serve some popcorn or seeded crackers.

Thanksgiving Pear Salad

One of the newer additions to Jessica's traditional feast, Jenny insists it be added to everyone's menu.

SERVES 15.

> 8 cups torn romaine or other lettuce
> 10 bosc pears, thinly sliced
> 1 cup feta cheese
> 2 cups finely chopped walnuts
> 1 cup fresh raspberries
> 1/2 cup raspberry vinegar
> 1/2 cup extra virgin olive oil
> 1 tsp salt
> 1 tsp pepper

On a large platter arrange romaine leaves and pear slices, then sprinkle the cheese, walnuts, and raspberries on top.

Place raspberry vinegar, olive oil, salt, and pepper in a jar and shake to combine. Drizzle over the salad.

Beet, Endive, and Goat Cheese Salad With Walnut Oil Vinaigrette

Add a Mediterranean flair to your feast with this tasty starter.

SERVES 6.

  4 ounces (1 cup) walnuts

  1 tbsp plus 1 tsp red wine vinegar

  1 tsp Dijon mustard

  1 shallot minced

  1/2 tsp salt

  1/4 tsp pepper

  2 1/2 tbsp walnut oil

  2 tbsp. olive oil

  1 16-ounce jar of beets, sliced

  2 pounds endive: 1 head separated into whole spears, the remainder sliced
    crosswise into 1/2-inch thick pieces

  4 ounces soft goat cheese

Toast the walnuts in a 350–degree F oven for 15 minutes until brown.

While the walnuts are toasting, whisk together the vinegar, mustard, shallot, salt, and pepper. Beat in the walnut oil and olive oil. Set aside for 10 minutes to blend flavors.

Cut the beets into wedges.

Decorate platter with whole endive in a circle. In large bowl toss sliced endive and 2 tbsp dressing. Mound on the platter. Add beets to remaining dressing, and scatter on salad.

Crumble goat cheese around the top and garnish with toasted walnuts.

Grandma Rose's "Green Salad"

❧❧

We can do without the turkey and maybe even skip the mashed potatoes, but no one is going to be happy if Grandma forgets to make her famous Green Salad.

1 3-ounce package lime Jell-O

1/2 cup sugar

3/4 cup boiling water

1/4 envelope, Knox gelatin

1 can crushed pineapple, drained

1 cup cottage cheese, small curd, low fat

1/2 cup chopped walnuts

1 cup Cool Whip

Combine the Jell-O, gelatin, sugar, and boiling water. Stir until the Jell-O and sugar dissolve, then cool.

Mix together the cooled Jell-O, crushed pineapple, cottage cheese, and nuts. When just ready to set, add Cool Whip whipped topping.

Pour into a mold and refrigerate to set.

BREADS

Yes, dinner rolls from the bakery make a fine accompaniment to your Thanksgiving meal, but why not jazz things up a bit with one of these flavorful recipes? In addition to adding spice to your Thanksgiving meal, they are a great morning snack for any guests who are staying overnight.

Pumpkin Bread

The perfect accompaniment to Thanksgiving breakfast, or you can use it as a dessert with coffee. From the kitchen of Rose Carroll.

MAKES 1 LOAF.

> 2 cups sifted flour
> 2 tsp baking powder
> 1/2 tsp baking soda
> 1 tsp cinnamon
> 1/2 tsp nutmeg
> 1 cup packed pumpkin (canned pumpkin is fine)
> 1 cup sugar
> 1/2 cup milk
> 2 eggs
> 1/4 cup soft butter
> 1 cup chopped pecans

Preheat oven to 350 degrees F.

Sift together the flour, baking powder, baking soda, cinnamon, and nutmeg.

Combine the pumpkin, sugar, milk and eggs in a large bowl. Slowly add dry ingredients and the butter. Mix until well blended. Stir in nuts.

Bake for 45–55 minutes or until a knife inserted into the middle of the loaf comes out clean.

Cranberry Nut Bread

Grandma Rose says this is the perfect treat for Thanksgiving breakfast.

MAKES 4 LARGE LOAVES.

    4 eggs, beaten
    4 oranges (make sure they are ripe and juicy)
    4 cups sugar
    1/2 cup melted margarine
    8 cups flour
    1 tsp salt
    6 tsp baking powder
    2 tsp baking soda
    4 cups cranberries
    2 cups chopped walnuts

Preheat oven to 325 degrees F.

Beat the eggs and set aside.

Squeeze the juice from the oranges into a measuring cup and add water to equal 3 cups. Add juice to eggs. Stir in sugar and margarine until well mixed. Slowly add flour, salt, baking powder, and baking soda. Mix until smooth.

Cut the cranberries into halves or quarters. Add cranberries and walnuts to batter.

Bake for 60–70 minutes or until a knife inserted into the middle of the loaf comes out clean.

Zucchini Bread

❖❖

If you're still wondering what to do with all those summer squash here's your answer. Great for breakfast and dinner.

MAKES 1 LOAF.

3 cups flour

2 tsp cinnamon

2 tsp nutmeg

1 tsp baking soda

1 tsp baking powder

1 tsp salt

3 eggs

1 cup sugar

1 cup vegetable oil

1 tbsp vanilla extract

3 cups grated zucchini

1 cup raisins

spray oil

Preheat oven to 350 degrees F.

In a mixing bowl, combine the flour, cinnamon, nutmeg, baking soda, baking powder, and salt.

In a separate, large bowl, beat the eggs. Add the sugar, vegetable oil, vanilla extract, and mix well.

Add the dry ingredients from above. Mix well.

Add the grated zucchini and raisins.

Pour into a loaf pan sprayed with oil. Bake for 1 hour or until a knife inserted into the middle of the loaf comes out clean.

You can also pour into sprayed and oiled muffin pans for delicious autumn muffins!

Orange Date Bread

❖❖

Breakfast, lunch or dinner, this delicious bread is perfect for any meal.

MAKES 1 LOAF.

$^1/_2$ cup boiling water

2 tbsp butter

2 tbsp grated orange rind

$^1/_3$ cup orange juice

$^1/_2$ cup finely chopped dates

1 cup sugar

$^1/_2$ tsp almond extract

1 egg, beaten

$^1/_2$ cup coarsely chopped walnuts

2 cups sifted flour

$^1/_4$ tsp baking soda

2 tsp baking powder

$^1/_2$ tsp salt

Preheat oven to 350 degrees F and butter bottom and sides of large loaf pan.

Place butter in a large mixing bowl and pour in boiling water. Stir until butter is melted. Add orange rind, orange juice, dates, sugar, almond extract, egg and nuts. Stir in sifted flour, baking soda, baking powder and salt. Mix well.

Pour dough into loaf pan and bake for 1 hour. Remove and cool on wire rack.

Popovers

These light and flaky rolls will thrill even the youngest guest. Serve with butter and honey for a special treat.

SERVES 8.

2 eggs beaten
1 cup milk
1 tbsp melted butter
1 cup flour
$\frac{1}{2}$ tsp salt

Preheat oven to 450 degrees and grease 8 custard cups.

Combine egg, milk and butter in small bowl. In larger bowl combine flour and salt. Make a hole in the dry ingredients and add the egg mixture. Stir just until the lumps disappear.

Fill custard cups until they are $\frac{1}{2}$–$\frac{1}{3}$ full. Bake for 15 minutes, then reduce heat to 325 degrees and bake for another 25 minutes.

When popovers are done, immediately remove from the pan so the steam doesn't soften them. Serve hot.

Ice Box Rolls

Not only are these rolls a delicious addition to your Thanksgiving meal, but they're guaranteed to make perfect sandwiches the next day.

MAKES A DOZEN MUFFINS.

2 cups hot water
$\frac{1}{2}$ cup shortening
$\frac{1}{2}$ cup sugar
2 packages dry yeast
1 tsp sugar
$\frac{1}{2}$ cup lukewarm water
2 eggs
8 cups flour
1 tbsp salt

Mix together hot water, shortening and sugar. Set aside to cool.

Dissolve the yeast and sugar in the lukewarm water. Add yeast mixture to first water mixture. Add eggs, salt and flour 1 cup at a time. When mixed well, place the dough in the refrigerator (ice box) until needed.

Just before dinner, preheat oven to 400 degrees. Remove dough from refrigerator and shape rolls. (This can be a terrific project for kids to use their imagination.) Allow rolls to rise to twice the size before baking.

Hint: For cloverleaf rolls, use a well-greased muffin tin and put three rounded pieces of dough in each cup. Let rise to double the size and bake for 10–15 minutes.

TURKEY

Of course no Thanksgiving is complete without a gigantic bird to grace your table. These days however, your turkey doesn't always have to be the "way grandma used to make it" to be delicious. Here you'll find not only a multitude of recipes for cooking the perfect bird, but tips and tricks to ensure it's juicy and delicious.

Buying the Turkey

One of the biggest questions people ask when getting ready for Thanksgiving is: How big does the turkey need to be? The standard rule of thumb is 1½ pounds of turkey per adult. If you have light eaters or are not concerned about leftovers, plan a pound for each person. For children, a half-pound per child should be plenty.

Thawing a Frozen Turkey

There are really three ways to thaw a frozen turkey: in the refrigerator, in the microwave, or by using cold water. If you chose to thaw under refrigeration, allow approximately 24 hours per 5 pounds. Therefore, if you have a 12-pound turkey, you should probably plan to put it in the refrigerator about 2½ days before Thanksgiving.

For cold water thawing, you need to put the turkey in a sink or pan of cold water and allow about 30 minutes per pound. Do *not* use warm or hot water and make sure you change the water every 30 minutes. A 12-pound turkey should take about 6 hours to thaw.

Thawing your turkey in the microwave means that you can begin to cook the turkey much quicker. However, it also means you have to have a microwave big enough to hold your turkey. To do so, follow the manufacturer's directions for your microwave.

Preparing the Turkey

One of the most common Thanksgiving stories isn't about the Pilgrims or Indians, but about how someone forgot to remove the neck and giblets. Before popping the bird in the oven, make sure to remove the neck from the body cavity and the giblets from the neck cavity. Then drain the juices and blot the cavities with paper towels.

If you plan to stuff your bird, which can be done only if you are roasting the turkey, be very careful not to stuff it too full. Stuffing the bird will significantly lengthen its cooking time, because the stuffing insulates the inside of the bird from the heat.

Deep-Fried Turkey

Deep-frying turkey is a Southern tradition that is slowly making its way north. While many people will cringe at the thought of deep-frying an entire turkey, those who've experienced it know that once you try it, you'll never go back. Not only does deep-frying take less than an hour to cook the entire bird, but it produces wonderfully juicy meat and a light crispy skin.

To make a deep-fried turkey, you will need a 40- to 60- quart pot with basket, burner and propane gas tank, a candy thermometer to measure oil temperature, and a meat thermometer to determine when the turkey is done. In addition, you will need a contraption to raise and lower the turkey in and out of the pot. Check out some of the Web sites and catalogs in Appendix A at the back of the book for suppliers. Otherwise you can create your own using heavy wire and a broom handle.

Safety Tip

Never fry or grill a turkey indoors, in a garage, or in any other structure attached to a building, or on a wooden deck— which could catch fire—or concrete—which can be stained by oil. Always place your fryer or grill on level dirt or a grassy area.

When choosing a turkey to fry, it is recommended that you find one between 8 and 15 pounds. Anything bigger will be awfully difficult to lift in and out of the pot.

Before you begin, it is important to determine how much oil you will need. To do this, put the turkey in the basket and place it in the pot. Add water until it is about 1 or 2 inches above the turkey. Remove the turkey and note the water level, using a ruler to measure the distance from the top of the pot to the surface of the water. Pour out the water and dry the pot thoroughly. For an 8- to 10-pound turkey or turkey parts, such as the breast, wings, or thighs, you will need approximately 5 gallons of oil.

Add the correct amount of oil to the pan and heat to 350 degrees. Depending on the amount of oil used, this usually takes between 45 minutes and 1 hour.

While the oil is heating, prepare the turkey as desired. Be sure to remove the neck and any giblets, and if the turkey comes with a built-in thermometer, remove that, too. Otherwise you could end up with deep-fried plastic.

Seasoning a fried turkey is much different from seasoning a grilled or roasted turkey. Traditionally, the turkey to be fried is injected with a liquid marinade, then the outside is rubbed with a dry rub. To properly season your turkey, place it in a pan and load your favorite marinade into a hypodermic meat injector. Inject the marinade in several places on the turkey. Rather than trying to poke the injector through the tough skin, carefully lift it up before injecting. When the turkey is good and loaded up with marinade, massage a big handful of dry rub onto the outside of the bird and all around the cavity.

WARNING: Do not stuff turkeys for deep-frying.

Once the oil has come to temperature (use a candy thermometer to test), place the turkey in the basket and slowly lower it into the pot. Before putting the turkey in the oil, though, it is important to make sure it is dry of all water and has been brought to room temperature. If you thawed it in cool water, make sure you use paper towels to thoroughly pat the turkey down.

Whole turkeys require approximately 3 minutes per pound to cook. Therefore, you can expect a 12-pound turkey to take about 35 minutes of cooking time. Once the time is up, remove the turkey and check the internal temperature with a meat thermometer by sticking the thermometer into the thigh and breast, being careful not to touch any bone. The temperature should reach 170 degrees F in the breast and 180 degrees F in the thigh.

When done, remove the turkey and let it stand 15 minutes before carving.

Grilled Turkey—on a Charcoal Grill

When you don't feel like slaving over a hot stove, a grilled turkey is the perfect solution. Whether you have a charcoal or gas grill, this is one of the best ways to prepare a juicy turkey with rich grilled taste. And it's probably pretty close to how the Pilgrims made their own Thanksgiving bird.

Prepare a charcoal-covered grill for Indirect Cooking Method (see your grill's cooking instructions) by removing the cooking grate and opening all vents. Position a drip pan in the middle of the charcoal grate and place twenty-five to thirty briquettes along each lengthwise side of the pan. Burn the briquettes until they are covered with a gray ash, about 30 minutes. When the charcoal is ready, place the cooking grate back in the grill.

Prepare a fresh or thawed turkey by removing the giblets and neck from the neck and body cavities, draining the juices and patting the turkey dry with paper towels. Do not stuff.

Turn the wings back to hold the neck skin in place. Return the legs to a tucked position if they are untucked. Brush the turkey, including the backside, with vegetable oil or spray completely with cooking spray. If desired, you can use a marinade on a grilled turkey. Do not use a turkey lifter when preparing a turkey for the grill.

Place the unstuffed turkey, breast up, on a cooking grate over the drip pan. Cover the grill, leaving vents open. Add six to eight briquettes, not infused with lighter fluid, to each side every 45 to 60 minutes.

Cook the turkey to an internal thigh temperature of 180 degrees F and breast temperature of 170 degrees F on a meat thermometer. A 10 to 18-pound turkey will take between 2 to 3 hours.

When done, remove the turkey from grill and let it stand 15 minutes before carving.

Wood-Smoked Turkeys on the Grill

If you'd like your turkey to have that wood-smoked flavor, try using wood instead of charcoal for your grilling. If you have a large grill, large pieces of wood should suffice. Heat the wood until you have a good bed of coals. If your grill is smaller, line the bottom of the grill with charcoal, and when the charcoal is red-hot, add the desired wood on top. Make sure that your grill is hot enough—the wood in a smaller grill might not reach the desired temperature and your turkey will cook forever!.

Here are some good choices of wood for grilling your Thanksgiving bird:

Alder	Maple
Apple	Hickory
Cherry	Pecan

Grilled Turkey—on a Gas Grill

Before you begin, make sure the turkey fits under the lid of your grill with at least 1 inch of space between the top of the turkey and the lid.

While the grill is still cool, lift the cooking grate and place a drip pan directly on either the flavorizer bars, ceramic briquettes, or lava rocks. Replace the cooking grate.

Prepare the grill for Indirect Heating Method according to the owner's guide for your grill. Preheat burners on HIGH for 10 to15 minutes with the lid closed.

Prepare a fresh or thawed turkey by removing the giblets and neck from the neck and body cavities, draining the juices and patting the turkey dry with paper towels. Do not stuff.

Turn the wings back to hold the neck skin in place. Return the legs to a tucked position if they are untucked. Brush the turkey, including the backside, with vegetable oil or spray completely with cooking spray. If desired, you can use a marinade on a grilled turkey. Do not use a turkey lifter when preparing a turkey for the grill.

Once the grill has been preheated, turn the temperature down to medium, or to a setting that maintains approximately 350 degrees F. Place the turkey, breast up, on the cooking grate over a drip pan. Close the lid and cook with minimal peeking.

Depending on your burner arrangement, it may be necessary to turn the turkey halfway around about midway through the cooking time so that both sides cook evenly. Cook the turkey to an internal thigh temperature of 180 degrees F and breast temperature of 170 degrees F on a meat thermometer. A 10- to 18-pound turkey will take between 2 to 3 hours.

When done, remove the turkey from the grill and let stand 15 minutes before carving.

Oven-Roasted Turkey

Once your turkey is thawed and your oven preheated to 325 degrees F, it is time to roast. If you plan on stuffing your turkey, now is the time. Carefully stuff the neck and body cavities lightly. Remember, if you stuff too full, you risk longer cooking time, since neither the stuffing nor the turkey will cook properly. Turn the wings back to hold the neck skin in place and return the legs to a tucked position if they are untucked. Contrary to what Grandma taught, it isn't necessary to truss your turkey. Trussing prevents hot air from circulating around the leg and thigh, meaning they won't cook at the same rate as the breast meat.

Make sure your roasting pan is at least 2 inches deep. Place the turkey, breast side up, on a flat rack in an open roasting pan. If you have a rack with a turkey lifter, be sure to use it. A lifter is a string cradle. When you place the turkey on the rack, you bring the loops around so it is easy to lift the turkey off the rack and out of the pan.

Turkey Tip

When choosing a pan to roast your turkey in, make sure it is a high-sided roasting pan with handles. The sides will prevent the juices from overflowing and making a mess in your oven, and the handles are crucial to helping you carry and move the heavy bird. Do *not* use a disposable or lightweight pan. Not only can they leak, but they are flimsy and can be dangerous when trying to lift your turkey from the oven.

If your turkey doesn't come with a gauge that pops when the meat reaches the proper temperature, you will need to insert an oven-safe meat thermometer. Make sure you stick it deep into the lower part of the thigh next to the body and not touching the bone.

Before placing the turkey in the oven, brush the skin with vegetable oil or butter to prevent it from drying. Basting is unnecessary and can actually dry out your turkey. Keeping your meat at a constant temperature will help it retain its moisture better than basting. The vegetable oil or butter will do the rest.

One of the best, but least practical, ways to ensure a moist turkey is to flip it over for the last 30 to 40 minutes of cooking. Let's face it, flipping a 16-pound bird is no easy task. Instead of flipping, place a piece of foil (or the lid of your pan) on top of the turkey for most of the cooking time. Remove the foil for the last 45 minutes of roasting to ensure browning.

Now it's time to sit and relax, or prepare the hundreds of other dishes you have planned. Don't even bother peeking at your turkey until about a half hour before you expect it to be done. Turkey is fully cooked when the thigh's internal temperature is 180 degrees F. The thickest part of the breast should be 170 degrees F, and the center of the stuffing should be 160 degrees F.

When done, let the turkey stand for 15 to 20 minutes before carving.

Turkey Roasting Chart for a 325-Degree Oven

Net Weight (in pounds)	Unstuffed (in hours)	Stuffed (in hours)
10 to 18	3 to 3½	3¾ to 4½
18 to 22	3½ to 4	4½ to 5
22 to 24	4 to 4½	5 to 5½
24 to 30	4½ to 5	5½ to 6¼

Tofu Turkey

Because not everyone shares a love for turkey, this vegetarian variation is bound to please all your meatless guests.

SERVES 4.

1 pound firm tofu
1 tsp salt
$^1/_4$ tsp dried marjoram
$^1/_4$ tsp dried savory
$^1/_4$ tsp pepper
$^1/_4$ cup margarine or butter
$^1/_2$ red onion, finely diced
$^1/_2$ cup celery
$^1/_4$ cup chopped mushrooms
1 clove garlic, minced
1 (12-ounce) package dry bread stuffing mix (unseasoned)
$^2/_3$ cup water
1 slice bread, cubed
$^1/_2$ tsp sage
$^1/_2$ tsp rosemary
$^1/_2$ tsp thyme
2 tbsp water
1 tsp BBQ sauce
$^1/_2$ tsp prepared mustard
1 tbsp orange jam
1 tsp orange juice
1 tbs sesame seeds
2 tbsp vegetable oil

Preheat oven to 400 degrees F.

Drain and rinse tofu; in a food processor or blender, process tofu until smooth. Stir in salt, marjoram, savory, and pepper. Line a strainer with cheesecloth and place over an empty bowl. Place tofu mixture in strainer and press against sides to form a deep well in the middle. Place more cheesecloth over tofu and refrigerate for 2 hours.

While the tofu is chilling, in a medium frying pan sauté

onion, celery, and mushrooms in butter until tender. Add garlic, ²/₃ cup water, salt and pepper to taste. Add stuffing mix, bring to a boil; reduce heat to low, cover, and simmer for 5 minutes. Remove from heat; let stand 5 minutes and fluff with a fork. To the stuffing, add bread cubes, sage, rosemary, thyme, and 2 tablespoons water.

After tofu has chilled for 2 hours, preheat oven to 350 degrees F. Spray baking sheet with vegetable spray or grease with vegetable oil.

Remove the top layer of cheesecloth from the tofu. If necessary, press tofu against the sides of the sieve to form a well. Spoon the stuffing mixture into the well and smooth the surface with a spoon. Invert the tofu mold onto a prepared baking sheet. Remove the remaining cheesecloth layer and shape the tofu with your hands if it has cracked or lost its shape.

Bake for 30 minutes.

Prepare the glaze by combining the barbecue sauce, mustard, orange jam, orange juice, sesame seeds, and oil. After tofu has baked for 30 minutes, brush or spoon the glaze over it. Return to the oven and bake for 20 minutes more.

When finished, broil for 3 to 5 minutes, or until tofu is browned and crispy.

Carving the Turkey

After all the work you've done to prepare the perfect Thanksgiving dinner, it would be a shame to destroy it all with improper carving. Whether you're doing the work yourself or leaving it up to someone else, here are tips to ensure that your turkey is carved in a way that preserves the flavor and texture of the meat.

Begin by choosing a sharp, thin-bladed carving knife. Running your knife along the bottom of the turkey, find the places where the thigh bones meet the body.

Slip your knife into the joint to separate the thigh from the body on each side.

Separate the drumstick from the thigh using the same technique (cut through the joint, not the bone, wiggling the drumstick to locate the joint). Running your knife along the bone, separate the meat from the thigh and drumstick—try to get as much as possible in one piece.

When the thigh and leg have been separated, you can either place them on the plate as is, giving some lucky people the chance to eat the leg whole, or cut the thigh and leg meat into thin slices.

Next, use your knife to find where the wings and body connect.

Slip your knife into the joint to separate the wings from the body on each side.

Carve thin slices off one side of the breast, cutting parallel to the breast.

Repeat with the other side of the breast.

Make a Wish!

Don't forget about your turkey wishbone! Take the turkey wishbone and dry it overnight. The day after Thanksgiving, two family members get to play Wishbone! Each person says a silent wish to herself and takes one side of the wishbone by curling it around the pinky finger. Both people pull and *snap!* Whoever gets the bigger piece has his or her wish come true!

VEGETABLES

Whether you eat them or not, it's a requirement to have vegetables alongside your potatoes, turkey, stuffing, pies, cranberries, and anything else you can squeeze on that table. While most of us traditionally stick with corn or green bean casserole, maybe this is the year to branch out. Instead of simply sticking with traditional, why not try one of these twists on an old veggie?

Nutty Lemon Green Beans

Erica Rose sends this as one of her favorite Thanksgiving vegetables.

SERVES 8.

> 2 pounds fresh green beans, trimmed and halved
>
> 5 tbsp butter
>
> 3/4 cup chopped pecans
>
> 4 tsp grated lemon peel
>
> 1/3 cup finely chopped fresh Italian parsley
>
> salt and pepper

Cook the beans in a large pot of boiling salted water until just tender, about 5 minutes. Drain and pat dry and allow to cool.

Melt the butter in a large deep skillet over medium heat. Add the pecans; sauté until nuts are crisp and butter is lightly browned, about 3 minutes. Add beans; toss to heat through, about 5 minutes. Mix in lemon peel; cook 1 minute. Mix in parsley. Season with salt and pepper. Transfer to bowl.

Lemony Artichokes

MAKES 2 SERVINGS.

2 whole artichokes
2 tbsp butter
juice from ¹/₂ lemon
salt and pepper to taste

Fill a large saucepan with just enough water to cover the bottom. Bring to a full boil over high heat. While the water is heating, trim and discard the stems and tough outer leaves of the artichokes.

When the water is boiling, place a steamer insert in the pot and set the artichokes in the steamer, stem side down. Cover the pot and allow the artichokes to steam for approximately 20 minutes, until tender.

When the artichokes are done, melt the butter and add the lemon juice. Eat artichokes by dipping leaves into lemon butter and scraping them with your teeth.

Confetti Corn

SERVES 8.

¹/₂ cup butter
2 tbsp minced green bell pepper
2 tbsp minced red bell pepper
2 tbsp all-purpose flour
2 (16-ounce) packages frozen corn kernels
1 pint half and half
1 pint heavy whipping cream
1 teaspoon salt
1¹/₂ tbs. granulated sugar
1 cup grated Romano cheese
²/₃ cup seasoned croutons
¹/₄ tsp ground black pepper

Preheat oven to 350 degrees F.
Lightly grease a 2-quart casserole dish.

In a large pot over medium heat, melt the butter. Slowly cook and stir the green bell pepper and red bell pepper until soft. Once soft, blend together with the flour.

Add the corn, half and half, whipping cream, salt, and sugar. Stir and heat until the mixture begins to thicken.

Stir in the cheese, seasoned croutons, and ground black pepper and pour into the baking dish. Bake uncovered in the preheated oven 40 minutes, until bubbly and lightly browned.

Candied Carrots

MAKES 4 SERVINGS.

1 pound carrots, cut into 2-inch pieces

2 tbsp butter, diced

1/4 cup packed brown sugar

1 pinch salt

1 pinch ground black pepper

Steam the carrots. Either use an electric steamer or steam by filling a medium saucepan with salted water so that the water just covers the bottom of the pan. Place the carrots in a steamer basket in the pot. Bring water to a boil, reduce the heat to a high simmer, cover, and cook about 20 to 30 minutes. Be careful not to overcook the carrots so they become mushy. The carrots should still be crisp.

Drain the water, reduce the heat to its lowest setting, and return the carrots to the pan. Stir in the butter, brown sugar, salt, and pepper. Cook for about 3 to 5 minutes, until the sugar is bubbly. Serve hot!

Your Quick Vegetable Cooking Guide

If you'd like to make some easy vegetables, here's a quick cooking guide to make your hectic day easier. Just add some butter, salt and pepper, or perhaps a little spice and you're ready to go. For instance, for tasty carrots, add some butter and nutmeg and you've got a delicious, easy side dish!

VEGETABLE	BOILING TIME
artichokes	40 minutes
asparagus	10–15 minutes
string beans	15–30 minutes
broccoli	10 minutes
brussels sprouts	20–30 minutes
cabbage	10–20 minutes
carrots, baby	10 minutes
cauliflower	10 minutes
corn kernels	5–8 minutes
corn on the cob	10–12 minutes
eggplant, whole	30 minutes
parsnips	25–35 minutes
peas	5–10 minutes
potatoes	20–40 minutes, depending on size
pumpkin	20–40 minutes
squash	20–40 minutes
turnips	20–40 minutes

VEGETABLE	STEAMING TIME
artichokes	50–60 minutes
asparagus	10–15 minutes
string beans	45–55 minutes
broccoli	10–15 minutes
cabbage	25 minutes
carrots, baby	35 minutes
cauliflower	10–15 minutes
parsnips	45–55 minutes
pumpkin	45 minutes
squash	45 minutes

VEGETABLE	BAKING TIME
beets	50 minutes @400 degrees
eggplant, sliced in half	35–45 minutes
parsnips	60–70 minutes
potatoes	45–60 minutes
pumpkin	60 minutes
squash	60 minutes
turnips	50-60 minutes

STUFFING AND POTATOES

Bring on the starch! No Thanksgiving meal is complete without heaping helpings of stuffing and mashed potatoes. However, if you're tired of the same old, same old, why not try something new? Cornbread dressing instead of Stouffer's or a stuffed acorn squash instead of traditional sweet potatoes. Whatever you do, make sure to leave plenty left over for some of the delicious leftover recipes later on.

Stuffing Warning

When stuffing your turkey, it is very important to be safe in order to prevent illness. Make sure that you stuff your turkey just before putting it in the oven. Leaving it out before cooking can cause harmful bacteria to build within your turkey's cavity.

To be fully cooked, your stuffing must reach 180 degrees (use a meat thermometer). If the turkey is done but the stuffing has not yet reached 180 degrees, remove the turkey, transfer the stuffing to a casserole dish, and return the stuffing to the oven to finish cooking.

For guaranteed safety, do not stuff your bird at all. Instead, make a traditional dressing—stuffing that is cooked outside the bird instead of in.

Frances Smythe Potts's Cornbread Dressing

Submitted by Aimee Schnabel who says her grandmother's recipe for cornbread dressing is the best. Served at both Thanksgiving and Christmas, this recipe includes notes from not only her grandmother but also Great-Aunt Jenne.

MAKES 2 PYREX DISHES (LONG).

5 cups cornbread, broken into small pieces
3 tbsp butter
¹/₂ cup finely chopped onions

2 cups chopped celery

3 garlic buttons (pressed)

1/4 cup minced parsley

1 1/2 cups green onions with tops

3 slices regular white bread, cubed

5 tbsp butter

1/4 cup onions (optional)

1 can chicken stock or broth

1/4 tsp cayenne pepper

Salt

Black pepper

Using a favorite recipe or box of cornbread mix (Aimee uses the recipe on the Magnolia Self-Rising Corn Meal bag), prepare the cornbread a day or two ahead of time if desired. It's actually better if the cornbread is a little stale, so don't worry about that.

Preheat oven to 350 degrees F.

Sauté onions, celery, garlic and parsley in 3 tbsps butter, then add to baking dish. In the same dish, crumble the cornbread and white bread together. Add cayenne pepper, salt, and pepper to taste (lots of pepper is better!). Dot the top with 5 tbsps butter. If you like the taste of onions, add 1/4 cup grated raw onions.

Add enough chicken stock to thoroughly soak all the bread. When you pat the top of the dish with a spoon little pools of stock should come to the top.

Bake for 25 minutes or longer if the stuffing seems too soupy. However, Aimee likes hers soft, like spoon bread.

Asian Rice Dressing

A melting-pot twist to a traditional American meal.

SERVES 15.

1 pound Italian turkey sausage links

2 cups chopped onion

Cooking oil

4 cups cooked rice

2 cups diced celery

8 cups bean sprouts

1 pound fresh mushrooms, sliced

2 (8-ounce) cans water chestnuts, drained

2 tsp poultry seasoning

1 tsp sage

Place the sausage and onion in a large, deep skillet. Cook over medium-high heat with oil until the sausage is cooked and the onions are translucent. Mix in the rice, celery, bean sprouts, mushrooms, water chestnuts, poultry seasoning, and sage. Cook until all ingredients are warmed through. When finished, place the dressing in a cheesecloth large enough that when filled with stuffing, it will fit inside the turkey cavity. Any remaining dressing may be put in cheesecloth and set alongside the turkey while baking. Keeping the cheesecloth and stuffing in the turkey pan allows it to absorb turkey drippings and adds more flavor.

Orange-Raisin Stuffing

✧✧

The perfect autumnal accompaniment to your feast.

SERVES 25.

1 cup raisins

1½ cups orange liqueur, such as Grand Marnier

1 cup unsalted butter

2 cups chopped celery

1 onion, chopped

1 pound spicy Italian sausage, casing removed

16 ounces herb-seasoned dry bread stuffing mix

1 cup chopped pecans

4 Granny Smith apples—peeled, cored, and chopped

2 cups chicken or turkey broth

4 tsp chopped fresh sage

salt and pepper to taste

Place the raisins in a small saucepan and cover with 1 cup of liqueur. Bring to a boil, remove from heat, and set aside.

In a large skillet, melt ¹/₂ the butter. Add the celery and onion and sauté over medium heat for 10 minutes. Transfer to a large mixing bowl. In the same skillet, cook the sausage over medium-high heat until crumbled and evenly brown. Remove from heat, drain, and combine in the bowl with the celery-onion mixture.

Add the stuffing mix to the vegetables and sausage. Stir in the raisins and liqueur; add pecans and apples, and combine thoroughly.

In a saucepan, melt the remaining ¹/₂ cup butter with the chicken or turkey broth. Pour over the stuffing along with the remaining ¹/₂ cup of orange liquer. Stir well, until moistened. Season with sage, salt, and pepper.

Garlic Mashed Potatoes

A snappy version of an old standby.

SERVES 12.

> 24 small red potatoes, peeled
> 1 head garlic
> olive oil
> ³/₄ cup butter
> salt to taste
> ¹/₂ tsp ground white pepper
> 1¹/₂ cups milk

Preheat oven to 350 degrees F.

Bring a large pot of water to a boil, add the potatoes, and let them boil until soft (approximately 25 minutes). Drain well.

While the water is boiling, brush the garlic with olive oil, wrap in foil, and place in 350-degree oven for 1 hour. When finished, gently squeeze the garlic out from each of the cloves, leaving behind the skins.

Place the potatoes, garlic pulp, butter, salt, pepper, and milk in a bowl. Blend until smooth or to your desired consistency.

Cheesey Mashed Potatoes

For those who think everything tastes better with a little cheese.

SERVES 8.

 1 pound potatoes
 ¹/₂ cup butter
 2 cups Parmesan cheese
 1 cup chopped fresh chives
 1¹/₂ cups cream cheese
 ¹/₂ medium head garlic
 salt and pepper to taste

Peel the potatoes. Cut into chunks of equal size. (The smaller the chunk, the quicker the cooking time.) Place potato chunks into a large pot and cover with cold water. Boil until tender but still firm.

Add the butter, cheese, chives, cream cheese, garlic, salt, and pepper. Beat until smooth and serve.

Honeyed Mashed Sweet Potatoes

This treat comes courtesy of JoAnne Murphy.

SERVES 12.

 12 sweet potatoes
 kosher salt, to taste
 ¹/₂ cup butter
 honey to taste
 cinnamon for garnish
 nutmeg for garnish

Peel the sweet potatoes. Cut into chunks of equal size (the smaller the chunk, the quicker the cooking time). Place the potato chunks into a large pot and cover with cold water. Boil until soft.

Drain the water and sprinkle the potatoes with kosher salt. Add the butter and mash until obtaining the desired smoothness. Mix in honey to sweeten to taste. Transfer to a large bowl and sprinkle with cinnamon or nutmeg before serving.

TIP: For smoother mashed potatoes, use your electric mixer. Creamy and smooth potatoes are one of the best Thanksgiving treats!

Sweet Potato Casserole

Although Thanksgiving isn't celebrated in England (for obvious reasons), Brit June Sach thinks her casserole recipe should be added to everyone's feast.

> 2 large sweet potatoes
> 1 cooking apple
> 3 carrots
> 1/2 tsp cinnamon
> 2 tbsp brown sugar
> 1/3 cup orange juice

Preheat oven to 350 degrees.

Slice the sweet potatoes, apple, and carrots. Combine the cinnamon and brown sugar. Layer sweet potatoes, carrots, and apple, and sprinkle combined sugar and cinnamon between layers.

Pour orange juice over the top. Bake for 1 hour or until soft.

Stuffed Acorn Squash

A terrific treat from JoAnne Murphy.

SERVES 8.

> 1 acorn squash
> 2 cooking apples
> 2 medium yellow onions
> 1 tbsp butter
> 1 cup finely chopped walnuts
> maple syrup
> brown sugar
> raisins (optional)

Preheat oven to 350 degrees F.

Cut the squash in half, lengthwise. Scrape out and discard the seeds. Spray a cookie sheet with nonstick spray and place the squash facedown on the cookie sheet. Bake for 25 to 30 minutes, depending on the size of the squash.

While the squash is baking, peel the apples and cut into small chunks. Chop the onions into very small pieces. Heat the butter in a frying pan and cook the onions and apples until soft. Add the walnuts and toss.

When the squash comes out of the oven, spoon the apple/onion/walnut mixture into the squash cavities. Drizzle with maple syrup and sprinkle with brown sugar. Return to oven and bake for approximately 30 more minutes. Keep an eye on it to ensure that it doesn't brown too much. Before serving, cut the halves into quarters. (Some folks like to sprinkle cheddar cheese on top and broil quickly before serving—an extra treat!)

NOTE: This squash is also delicious prepared with no stuffing—just bake facedown for half an hour, flip over, drizzle with melted butter, maple syrup, or honey, and brown sugar and bake face up for 30 more minutes. YUM!

SUBSTITUTION: Honey may be substituted for maple syrup in this recipe.

GRAVIES AND SAUCES

While the turkey is essential to a Thanksgiving meal, the meal just isn't complete without the gravy and cranberry sauce, too. Sure, you can always buy them in a jar or can, but aren't they a whole lot better homemade? In the following pages you'll find not only traditional recipes for gravy and other sauces, but also some new twists that will leave your mouth watering just reading the ingredients.

Classic Turkey Gravy

❖❖

An excellent recipe for using those turkey drippings!

MAKES 4 CUPS.

Milk or canned turkey or chicken broth
¹/₂ cup flour or ¹/₄ cup cornstarch
Turkey giblets (if desired)

Pour turkey drippings from the pan into a 4-cup measuring cup. Remove ¹/₄ cup of the fat from the top of the drippings in your measuring cup. Place the drippings back into the roasting pan. Use a piece of bread (the heel works nicely) to soak up the remaining fat on the top of your measuring cup. Simply place the bread on top of the drippings and toss out when soaked. Add broth or milk to the drippings in the measuring cup until it equals 4 cups.

Using a whisk, blend ¹/₂ cup flour (¹/₄ cup cornstarch) with the fat in the pan. Gradually blend in liquid from the measuring cup until smooth. Bring to a boil, stir, and simmer about 5 minutes. Add finely chopped cooked giblets, if desired.

Turkey Giblet Gravy

A very traditional gravy like the one grandma used to make.

3 tbsp turkey drippings
3 tbsp all-purpose flour
2¹/₂ cups turkey (or chicken) stock

¹/₂ tbsp chopped fresh sage

¹/₂ tsp ground black pepper

salt to taste

¹/₄ cup turkey giblets

Heat pan drippings in a large skillet over medium heat. Gradually add flour and stir until golden brown.

Slowly add the turkey stock, stirring with a whisk until blended. Add the sage, pepper, salt, and giblets. Bring to a boil, then remove from heat and serve warm.

Cranberry Turkey Gravy

A delicious combination of sauces that will add zing to your feast.

3¹/₂ tbsp turkey pan drippings

3¹/₂ tbsp flour

1¹/₄ cups canned chicken or turkey broth

¹/₄ cup cranberry juice

¹/₂ cup whole berry cranberry sauce

salt and freshly ground pepper to taste

Heat pan drippings in a large skillet over medium heat. Add the flour, stirring continually with a whisk; cook for 1 minute, being careful not to let the flour mixture brown. Slowly whisk in the chicken or turkey broth until smooth. Whisk in the cranberry juice and continue to stir until the mixture comes to a boil and thickens.

Reduce heat to low and stir in the cranberry sauce until incorporated. Season the gravy to taste with salt and pepper. Keep warm over very low heat until ready to serve.

Vegetarian Gravy

Because while not everyone will eat turkey gravy, almost everyone likes gravy on their mashed potatoes.

MAKES 8 CUPS.

> $\frac{1}{2}$ cup vegetable oil
> 5 cloves garlic, minced
> $\frac{1}{3}$ cup chopped onion
> $\frac{1}{2}$ cup all-purpose flour
> 4 tsps nutritional yeast
> 4 tbsp light soy sauce
> 2 cups vegetable broth
> $\frac{1}{2}$ tsp sage
> $\frac{1}{4}$ tsp ground black pepper
> $\frac{1}{2}$ tsp salt
> 4 tsps all-purpose flour

In a saucepan over medium to low heat, combine the oil, garlic, and onion; cook until onion is translucent.

Add the flour, yeast, and soy sauce to make a paste. Gradually mix in the broth, stirring constantly, followed by the seasonings.

Cranberry-Apple Sauce

The perfect sauce for anyone watching sugar or calorie intake.

> 12 ounces cranberries
> 6 ounces unsweetened apple juice concentrate

In a saucepan cook cranberries and apple juice concentrate over medium heat until cranberries have burst. Chill and serve.

Cranberry Chutney

Originally from India, Chutney is condiment similar to cranberry sauce or salsa. This version has more spices than cranberry sauce.

MAKES 2 CUPS.

1 package (12 ounces) fresh cranberries
½ cup balsamic vinegar
½ cup sugar
1 tsp nutmeg
1 tsp cinnamon
1 tsp cayenne pepper
1 tsp cumin

In a medium saucepan over high heat, combine the cranberries, vinegar, and sugar; bring to a boil.

Reduce the heat to medium-low and add nutmeg, cinnamon, cayenne, and cumin.

Simmer for 20 to 25 minutes or until the mixture is very thick, stirring frequently. Chill before serving.

Aunt Ellain's Good Cranberry Relish

Contributed by Kim Knowles DeRoche.

2 (3-ounce) packages of orange Jell-O
1 cup boiling water
1 cup sugar
1 cup orange juice
1 pound ground cranberries

Combine Jell-O, water, and sugar in a large bowl. Allow to cool. Then, add orange juice and cranberries. Pour into a gelatin mold, stir a couple of times, and chill.

BONUS: Add chopped nuts or chopped apples for a delicious variation!

DESSERT

No Thanksgiving meal is complete without plenty of dessert. An apple pie from Grandma? Dad's favorite pecan and your own chocolate creation are a must. Whether you're looking for the perfect pie recipe or want to add a new treat to your meal, you're bound to find at least one new family favorite in this list. From tips on making a perfect pie crust to a chocolate pecan pie—a twist on an old favorite, there's something here for everyone.

Grandma's Pie Crust

Whether you use your grandma's or your neighbor's, everyone has a favorite pie crust. Use this for all the pies listed in this section, or use your favorite store-bought crust (we won't let anyone in on your secret).

MAKES ONE PIE CRUST (BOTTOM ONLY). DOUBLE THE RECIPE FOR A TOP LAYER.

  1 cup all-purpose flour
  ¹/₈ tsp salt
  ¹/₃ cup butter, chilled
  3 tbsp cold water

Stir together the flour and salt in a large bowl. Cut in the butter until crumbly. Mix in just enough water, with a fork, only until the flour is moistened. Shape dough into a ball. Flatten the ball.

Roll out the dough on a lightly floured surface into 12-inch circle. Place in 9-inch pie pan. Crimp or flute the edge. Set aside while you make the pie filling of your choice.

Classic Pumpkin Pie

No Thanksgiving is complete without one.

  2 eggs
  1 cup firmly packed brown sugar
  ¹/₂ cup heavy whipping cream

1 (15-ounce) can pumpkin

1 tsp pumpkin pie spice

$^1/_2$ tsp salt

1 unbaked 9-inch pie crust

SPICED WHIPPED CREAM

$^1/_2$ cup heavy whipping cream

1 tbsp sugar

$^1/_4$ tsp ground cinnamon

Preheat oven to 425 degrees F.

Beat eggs at medium speed with a large mixer until thick and lemon-colored (2 to 3 minutes). Add all remaining filling ingredients; beat until well mixed (1 to 2 minutes).

Pour the filling into the prepared pie crust. Bake for 10 minutes. Reduce oven temperature to 350 degrees F. Continue baking for 40 to 50 minutes or until knife inserted in center comes out clean. Cool completely.

Beat $^1/_2$ cup chilled whipping cream at high speed in a small chilled mixing bowl, scraping the bowl often, until soft peaks form. Add the sugar and cinnamon. Continue beating until stiff peaks form (1 to 2 minutes).

To serve, top each serving with a dollop of whipped cream. Sprinkle with additional ground cinnamon, if desired. Store pie and whipped cream refrigerated.

Chocolate Pecan Pie

A delicious twist on an old American favorite.

1 (9-inch) unbaked pie crust

3 eggs

$^2/_3$ cup white sugar

$^1/_2$ tsp salt

$^1/_3$ cup margarine, melted

1 cup light corn syrup

1 cup pecan halves

$1^1/_2$ cups semisweet chocolate chips

Preheat oven to 375 degrees F. Prepare the pie shell.

Beat the eggs, sugar, salt, margarine, and syrup with a hand beater. Stir in the pecans and chocolate chips. Pour into the pie shell.

Bake until set, 40 to 50 minutes. Let cool before cutting.

Getting your pastry perfect is not always easy for those new to pie-making. Use this handy trouble-shooting list to ensure your Thanksiving pies leave them coming back for more!

The Pastry Trouble Shooter

Problem:	Solution:
My pastry crumbles!	Your pastry could be too cold. Try leaving it on the counter for a few minutes. Or it could be too dry—add a few more drops of water. You could also be overmixing the butter and the flour—cut back next time.
My pastry doesn't brown!	Use a Pyrex or enamel pie pan and bake at a constant temperature.
My pastry is tough!	You are probably using too much water. Cut back. You could also be overmixing. Just mix enough to get all the ingredients together. Then back off.
Help! My pastry sticks to the rolling pin!	Have you floured the rolling pin and the counter? If this doesn't work, try chilling the pastry for a little while.
My pastry edges burn!	Cover the edge of the pie plate and crust with aluminum foil. Remove 15 minutes before you are finished baking so it browns nicely.
My crust isn't nice and flaky!	Are you using chilled butter? Make sure the water you are using is also chilled. Good luck!

Original Apple Pie

No Thanksgiving is complete without this all-American specialty.

2 9-inch unbaked pie crusts

³/₄ cup white sugar

2 tbsp all-purpose flour

¹/₂ tsp ground cinnamon

¹/₄ tsp ground nutmeg

¹/₂ tsp lemon zest

7 cups thinly sliced apples (Granny Smith or Macintosh work best)

2 tsp lemon juice

1 tbsp butter

4 tbsp milk (optional)

Preheat oven to 425 degrees.

Mix together the sugar, flour, cinnamon, nutmeg, and lemon zest, set aside.

Line one crust in a 9-inch deep-dish pie pan. Layer ¹/₃ of the apples into the pie crust. Sprinkle with sugar mixture and repeat until done. Sprinkle with lemon juice and dot with butter.

Place second pie crust on top of filling and flute the edges. Cut vents in top crust and brush with milk for a glazed appearance if desired.

Bake at 425 degrees for 40 to 50 minutes.

Nutty Coffee

J ust before making a fresh pot of coffee, sprinkle cinnamon, nutmeg, or pumpkin pie spice into the coffee filter with the ground coffee beans. The spicy flavor will warm the hearts and hands of all your guests.

Heaven's Cake

This Chocolate Cookie Cake, from Nanny Sach, is an old family recipe that is sure to knock your socks off. It's rich, so take it easy or suffer the consequences.

> 8 ounces unsweetened chocolate (Hershey's Special Dark)
> 8 ounces butter (or margarine)
> 2 eggs
> 2 heaping tbsp sugar
> 2 drops vanilla essence
> 8 ounces biscuits (such as plain tea biscuits) broken into small pieces (about ½-inch)
> chopped nuts (optional)

Slowly melt the chocolate and butter in the top of a double boiler or in a microwave oven.

Beat the eggs and sugar together. Slowly add the chocolate and butter, a little at a time, beating the ingredients together. Add the vanilla and broken-up biscuits and stir. Add nuts if desired.

Pour into a buttered loaf pan and refrigerate at least 2 days. (You may want to put a lock on the fridge door for 2 days as temptation might urge someone to sample earlier. Follow the fudge fingerprints to uncover the culprit!)

Grandma Lila's Carrot Bars

A favorite of old and young, and especially Jessica.

> 4 eggs
> 2 cups sugar
> ¾ cup vegetable oil
> 2 jars (junior size) carrot baby food
> 2 cups flour
> 2 tsp baking soda
> ½ tsp cinnamon
> 1 tsp vanilla extract
> 1 cup chopped walnuts

FROSTING

2 tbsp butter

1–3 ounces cream cheese

2 cups powdered sugar

vanilla extract to taste

Preheat oven to 350 degrees F.

Beat together eggs, sugar, oil, and baby food. When combined, slowly add in flour, baking soda, cinnamon, and vanilla until mixed. Then add nuts as desired.

Place batter in a 15-by-10 inch jelly roll pan. Bake for 30 minutes.

When done, set bars out to cool while you make the frosting: Combine all the frosting ingredients and beat well until smooth and creamy. Frost on warm carrot bars.

Amy Z's Pumpkin Bread Pudding

A yummy alternative to pumpkin pie from Amy Zavatto.

³/₄ cup sugar

¹/₂ tsp salt

¹/₂ tsp ginger

¹/₄ tsp nutmeg

1¹/₂ tsp ground cinnamon

¹/₄ tsp ground clove

1¹/₂ cups cooked, pureed pumpkin (You can use the canned, but we prefer using the real stuff!)

3 eggs

1¹/₂ cups half and half

3 tbsp dark, sweet rum

1 loaf stale or toasted semolina Italian bread (sesame seeds are okay)

Preheat oven to 350 degrees F.

Combine the sugar, salt, spices, and pumpkin in a large bowl. In a separate bowl, beat together the eggs, cream, and rum. When well mixed, add to the dry ingredients.

Cut the bread into 1- to 1¹/₂-inch cubes. Place the bread pieces into a deep (you know, the really big one) Corningware dish. Pour the pumpkin mixture over the top. Bake for 30 minutes, or until it becomes stiff (but not burned!). Serve with fresh whipped cream.

Old-Fashioned Pumpkin Cookies

Kris Curry doesn't do much cooking, but when she whips up a batch of these pumpkin cookies, everyone is begging for more.

MAKES 3 DOZEN COOKIES.

2½ cups all-purpose flour
1 tsp baking soda
1 tsp baking powder
1 tsp ground cinnamon
½ tsp nutmeg
½ tsp salt
½ cup butter, softened
1½ cups granulated sugar
1 cup solid packed pumpkin
1 egg
1 tsp vanilla extract
Glaze (recipe follows)

GLAZE

2 cups powdered sugar
3 tbsp milk
1 tbsp butter
1 tsp vanilla extract

Preheat oven to 350 degrees F.

Combine the flour, baking soda, baking powder, cinnamon, nutmeg, and salt in a medium bowl. Cream the butter and sugar in large mixing bowl. Add the pumpkin, egg, and vanilla. Beat until light and creamy. Mix in the dry ingredients until well blended.

Drop by rounded tablespoon onto a greased cookie sheet. Smooth the tops of the cookies.

Bake for 15 to 20 minutes. Cool on wire racks.

To make glaze: Sift the powdered sugar. Melt the butter in a microwave or on the stovetop. Combine all ingredients and mix until smooth.

Drizzle glaze over the top of cookies.

NOTE: For variation, stir any one of the following ingredients into the batter:

1 cup raisins

1 cup chopped nuts

1 cup rolled oats

$^1/_2$ cup crushed pineapple, drained

1 cup dried cranberries

1 cup chocolate chips (no glaze)

24-Carat Cake

A terrific recipe from Erica Rose Tickle who was kind enough to share this special family secret.

8 medium carrots

2 cups flour

2 tsp baking powder

$^1/_2$ tsp baking soda

$^1/_4$ tsp salt

$^1/_2$ tsp mace

1 tsp cinnamon

1 cup butter

1 cup brown sugar

1 cup sugar

4 eggs, separated

1 cup chopped walnuts

GOLDEN CARROT FROSTING

$^1/_4$ cup butter, at room temperature

2 cups powdered sugar, sifted

$^1/_4$ cup reserved cooked carrots

2 tbsp orange juice

$1^1/_2$ tsp grated fresh orange peel

Preheat oven to 350 degrees F.

Peel and slice the carrots. Cook covered until very tender, in 1 cup water. Drain, reserving $1/3$ cup of the cooking liquid. Puree the carrots in a blender (or use a potato masher). There should be 1 cup of puree. Use $3/4$ cup puree for the cake and reserve $1/4$ cup for the frosting.

Sift together the flour, baking powder, baking soda, salt, and spices.

Cream butter and sugars together until light and fluffy. Beat in the egg yolks one at a time.

Blend in the dry ingredients, $1/3$ at a time, alternating with the carrot puree and carrot liquid. Stir in the nuts.

Beat the egg whites until stiff and gently fold into batter. Spread in a greased and floured $9 \times 13 \times 2$-inch baking pan.

Bake for 45 minutes. Cool for 10 minutes and turn out onto a wire rack to cool completely.

To make frosting: Cream the butter until soft and gradually beat in the powdered sugar, alternating with cooked carrots and orange juice.

When smooth and fluffy, stir in grated orange peel.

Allow cake to cool completely before frosting.

LEFTOVERS

One of the greatest things about Thanksgiving is the leftovers. Of course, sometimes they are the worst part of Thanksgiving. After all, how many turkey sandwiches can a person eat? Well, lucky for you we've got a solution to the great American leftover problem. Here you'll find a collection of delicious recipes to get your family eating that day-old turkey and potatoes. In fact, we guarantee they'll like them so much you'll be making turkey year-round just for the leftovers.

Turkey and Potato Casserole

Whether you're looking for a delicious side dish or the perfect post-Thanksgiving meal this dish is sure to please the smallest to the oldest and can be easily made to accommodate any leftover foods.

SERVES 10.

- 2 (2-pound) packages frozen hash brown potatoes
- 1/2 cup chopped onion
- 2 (10³/4-ounce) cans condensed cream of chicken soup
- 1 (10³/4-ounce) can condensed cream of mushroom soup
- 2 tbsp chopped fresh chives
- 1/4 pound butter, melted
- 1 (8-ounce) container sour cream
- 1/2 cup shredded cheddar cheese
- 2 cups shredded leftover turkey (or to taste)
- 1/2 cup crushed potato chips or bread crumbs

Preheat oven to 350 degrees F.

In a 6-quart casserole dish, mix together all the ingredients except the potato chips. Bake the casserole covered for 45 minutes.

Uncover, sprinkle with potato chips, and bake for an additional 15 to 25 minutes or until the casserole has just begun to bubble around the edges.

Pilgrim's Pie

If the Pilgrims had been Irish you can guarantee we would all be eating this delicious version of their famous shepherd's pie. Not only is it a great way to use leftovers, but it's a terrific comfort food for those cold winter days.

SERVES 6.

2 pounds potatoes
2 tbsp butter
¼ cup milk
    (or 2 pounds of leftover mashed potatoes)
3 onions
1 pound leftover turkey, cut into small pieces
1 (10-ounce) package frozen green peas, thawed
1 (10-ounce) package frozen corn kernels
    (or the leftover corn from your dinner)
1 tbsp paprika
1 pinch ground nutmeg
1 pinch dried sage
1 pinch salt
1 pinch ground black pepper

Preheat oven to 400 degrees F.

If you aren't planning to use those leftover mashed potatoes, you will need to boil the potatoes until tender. Mash them with milk and 2 tablespoons butter or margarine. Season with nutmeg, salt and pepper. Set aside.

Sauté the onions with the paprika. Add the leftover turkey and sage, and toss until the turkey is well coated.

In a sauce pan, blanch the frozen vegetables for 5 minutes in boiling water. Drain.

Spread a thin layer of potatoes in the casserole dish. Add half the peas and corn, then the turkey, then the rest of the peas and corn. Top with mashed potatoes.

Dot the top with flakes of butter, nutmeg, paprika, salt and pepper. Bake for 40 to 50 minutes, or until golden brown.

Turkey Enchiladas

❖❖

Olé! When you've had enough of good-old American cooking, it's time to add a little spice to your meal plan. These quick and easy enchiladas prove what a melting pot America is by taking the leftovers from your all-American meal and giving them a Mexican twist.

SERVES 6.

1 (10-ounce) can enchilada sauce

1 10³/₄-ounce) can condensed cream of mushroom soup

1 (7-ounce) can diced green chiles

2 cups shredded turkey

2 cups grated cheddar cheese

10 large flour tortilla shells

Preheat oven to 350 degrees F.

In a small bowl, mix together enchilada sauce and mushroom soup. Set aside.

Place each tortilla shell flat on the counter and fill with one heaping teaspoon each of the green chilies, turkey, and cheese. Roll and place in a 9- × 11-inch pan. Continue until the tortillas fill the pan. Pour your sauce mixture over the tortillas, being careful that each one is thoroughly covered.

Cover the pan with foil and bake for 30 minutes or until your enchiladas are cooked through.

If desired, serve with sour cream, guacamole, diced tomatoes, and shredded lettuce.

Stuffkey Bake

So many leftover recipes call for potatoes or turkey, but what the heck should you do with all that leftover stuffing? This yummy recipe easily answers that question for you. So bake and enjoy!

SERVES 4 TO 6.

> 3 cups leftover stuffing
> 2³/₄ ounces French fried onions
> 1 (10³/₄-ounce) can condensed cream of celery soup
> ³/₄ cup milk
> 1¹/₂ cup leftover turkey, cut up into bite-sized pieces
> 1 (10-ounce) package frozen green corn, thawed

Preheat oven to 350 degrees F.

Mix the stuffing together with the ¹/₂ can of onions. Press it into the bottom and sides of a 9-inch shallow baking dish. The mixture should form a shell on the bottom of the pan.

Combine soup, milk, turkey, and peas; pour into stuffing shell.

Cover the pan and bake for 30 minutes. Top with the remaining onions and bake uncovered for an additional 5 minutes.

Family Favorites

Everyone has favorite recipes that are eaten only on Thanksgiving. Make sure yours don't get lost to the ages—jot them down here to share with generations to come.

RECIPE ——————————————————————

SERVES ——————————

————————————————————————————

————————————————————————————

————————————————————————————

————————————————————————————

————————————————————————————

————————————————————————————

————————————————————————————

————————————————————————————

————————————————————————————

————————————————————————————

————————————————————————————

✤✤

RECIPE ——————————————————————

SERVES ——————————

————————————————————————————

————————————————————————————

————————————————————————————

————————————————————————————

————————————————————————————

————————————————————————————

————————————————————————————

————————————————————————————

————————————————————————————

————————————————————————————

————————————————————————————

RECIPE _____

SERVES _____

_____
_____
_____
_____
_____
_____
_____
_____
_____
_____
_____
_____

✤✤

RECIPE _____

SERVES _____

_____
_____
_____
_____
_____
_____
_____
_____
_____
_____
_____
_____
_____

RECIPE _____

SERVES _____

_____
_____
_____
_____
_____
_____
_____
_____
_____
_____
_____
_____
_____
_____

✦✦

RECIPE _____

SERVES _____

_____
_____
_____
_____
_____
_____
_____
_____
_____
_____
_____
_____
_____
_____

4

Setting the Feast

One cannot think well, love well, sleep well, if one has not dined well.
—*Virginia Woolf*

*F*or many, an attractive table is easy—add some candles and let the turkey act as centerpiece. For others, creating centerpieces and place cards is an art. Just look at some of the creations of Martha Stewart. While we aren't expecting you to be Martha, we are giving you a number of ideas and suggestions to make your table special each year. Some are more complicated and take advance planning, while others are great craft ideas for kids.

Pick and choose the centerpiece that most fits your meal, as well as some of the suggestions we have made for outdoor and indoor decorations. After all, there's no reason you can't extend your Thanksgiving arrangements beyond the table.

Setting the Table

For many, Thanksgiving is one time of year when the good china and linens come out of the closet. It is also a time to brush up on setting a proper table, not easy if you're used to eating pizza from the box on a regular basis.

It is tricky enough to remember where to put the knife, fork, and spoon, but add to that two glasses, three plates, and a cup and saucer, and even the best maître d' will often shake his head in confusion.

The best way to plan your table setting is to start from the center and work your way out. That means plates. Obviously your dinner plate goes first. If you have a charger that should go under the dinner plate, although few people actually use chargers these days.

An oversized dinner plate, a charger is essentially a decorative item. Its primary job is to sit under the dinner plate and add pizzazz to the table. The charger should always be removed before dinner is served.

The side plate or salad plate should be placed directly to the left of the place setting and the bread and butter plate should be placed just above the forks.

When placing silverware on the table, it is important to remember one key rule: Place them in the order you will use them, from the outside in. Forks should go on the left and spoons and knives on the right. Spoons and knives are to be placed together with knife blades pointing toward the plate. Fork prongs should point upward.

From the outside in, forks should be placed in the following order: salad fork, dinner fork, and dessert fork if necessary. Spoons should go on the outside of the knife (assuming you are having soup).

If possible, it is best to leave forks or spoons for dessert in the kitchen. This will keep the clutter down and eliminate washing clean silver.

Wineglasses should be placed at the tip of the main-course knife. If there is more than one glass (wine or water), arrange them in the order they'll be used, outermost first. Coffee cups and saucers can be placed directly to the right of the place setting; however, to keep clutter down at the table, it might be best to leave them in the kitchen until dessert is served. As a general rule, items used for liquids—such as glasses—go on the right. Dry items—such as salad plates—go on the left!

If you are going to fold the napkin in one of the fancy designs we talk about later, you can place it on top of the main plate. Otherwise, the napkin can be placed on the side plate or to one side of the glasses.

Setting the Buffet

With larger families and a growing crowd at Thanksgiving, it might be easier for you to forgo the formal sit-down meal and head for the buffet table. But just because you are doing a buffet doesn't mean you have to give up an attractive table.

One of the key ingredients to building a beautiful buffet table is elevation. Don't just throw all your platters and bowls on the table; give them some height. Use blocks of wood, upside-down bowls, upside-down flowerpots, or anything else you can find to put your serving platters of turkey and bowls of mashed potatoes on. Just make sure the block is sturdy enough that your bowl is secure and won't topple once people dip the serving spoon in.

The best way to put the table together is to find a tablecloth that is too big for your buffet table (use two tablecloths if necessary). Place your elevation stands under the cloth so they are hidden. Obviously the bowls and platters at the back of the table should be raised and the ones in front can actually be sitting on the table itself.

And don't forget decoration. Buy some cut flowers, gather dry some leaves, or tuck bunches of acorns in those spaces between bowls to give your table some color.

Dressing the Table

When planning your table, it is important to remember that what goes under your place setting is just as important as the china itself.

If you're lucky enough to have a beautiful table, you might want to consider putting away the tablecloth and using place mats instead. Not only are they a great way to individualize each person's place, but they can really be fun and different. Instead of the same old white cloth, you can get place mats made from rush, wood, or even brightly colored fabrics. Consider mixing and matching some of the place mats you already have, or get the kids together to make a special place for everyone.

Place mats are easy to make. Begin by drying a bunch of leaves following the directions for the Leafy Table. Once dried, place the leaves between a colored backing (construction paper works well) and a piece of clear Contac paper. These original place mats will make everyone smile when they sit down to dinner.

For the more traditional approach, or if you are concerned about the damage hot plates and little fingers can cause, a tablecloth is probably the way to go. But don't feel as if you have to use the same white linen your mother and grandmother used. Get creative. What about an orange or brown cloth to celebrate the season or one with leaves embroidered into the cloth?

If you don't have the money to buy a brand-new tablecloth, go to the nearest fabric store and buy an inexpensive piece of autumnal-colored cloth. You can either place it over an existing cloth or use it on its own.

Just keep in mind that patterns can be tricky. If you have patterned china or plan to have an elaborate centerpiece, it might be best to stick with a simple tablecloth or place mats.

Napkins

There is nothing wrong with using paper napkins for Thanksgiving (especially if you have a lot of people or you really liked the turkey design you found), but for those who really want an elegant dinner, cloth is the way to go. If you decide to use one of the fancy folds below, you should be sure that your napkins are well starched and can hold their shapes without wire support.

Pocket Fold

1. Begin with your napkin flat in front of you.
2. Fold the napkin in half horizontally, with the open side facing you.
3. Fold up about 2 inches of the bottom of the upper layer.
4. Fold it up once again.
5. Flip the napkin over so your folded side is now on the bottom.
6. Bring each edge in to the center of the napkin.
7. Fold in half along the center.
8. Turn the napkin over and you have a perfect pocket.

Pyramid Fold

1. Begin with your napkin flat in front of you.
2. Fold the napkin diagonally, with the point of the triangle facing you.
3. Fold the bottom (the point) of the napkin to the top (the creased edge), so that the point now touches the crease.
4. Take each side and fold it down, evenly along the middle section, so that the point of each side is pointing toward you.
5. Turn the napkin (from side to side, not up or down) over and fold the flaps up to make a smaller triangle.
6. Fold the napkin along the central axis and stand up in a triangle.

Corn Fold

1. Fold the napkin in half diagonally, with the center point facing away from you.
2. Bring the ends up over to the middle and on top of the center point.
3. Turn the napkin over and fold the bottom up about halfway.
4. Bring each side in to the center.
5. Turn the napkin over and fold the bottom up about 1 inch.
6. Fold the napkin in half along the central axis, with the bottom fold on the outside.
7. Loosely pull open the "skin" of the corn.
8. Place the napkin in a wine or water glass.

Place Cards

Once the table is set, it is time to figure out who is going to be sitting where. Whether you have four or fourteen people, using place cards can help you avoid those awkward moments when everyone wants to sit next to Sweet Aunt Sally, but avoids Cranky Uncle Carl like the plague. Place cards can be as easy or as complicated as you want them to be. Use your imagination, or some of the creative ideas below.

- Buy unlined index cards, fold them in half, and use your best handwriting to fill in the names. If you'd like, use stickers of pumpkins, turkeys, or leaves to add an autumnal touch.
- Gourds can make great place cards. Buy a selection of different gourds (making sure you have one for every guest and a few extras for emergencies). Use twine, raffia, or other ribbon to tie around the top of the gourd and a permanent marker to write the guest's name. If you'd like, allow the kids to be creative. Add faces, construction paper hats, or even legs and arms.
- Miniature pumpkins or apples make very attractive and seasonal place card holders. Simply cut a slit in an apple or a miniature pumpkin and slip in the card.
- Use potted plants as place card holders and favors for your guests to take home. Buy miniature chrysanthemums or another flowering plant. Place each pot in a brown paper bag with the top rolled down and tie off with ribbons. Then use your imagination to decorate the bags and write the name of each guest on a bag.
- Another great place card idea: Leaves make great decorations and tend to be easily found this time of year. Collect and dry a variety of fallen autumn leaves in different colors. Using a paint pen, write each guest's name on a leaf at his or her place.
- Glue an oak leaf and a couple of small acorns onto a plain card (spray-painted metallic gold or copper if desired).
- Give the kids something to do while you're preparing the turkey. Buy prefolded cards from a craft or party store

and pass out markers, a list of names, and stickers. Everyone will be thrilled with a very personal place card. If the kids are too young to write the names, simply fill them all in before handing them off.

- Pinecones make perfect place card holders. Write each guest's name on a small piece of paper and nestle it between the spaces of a pinecone.

Drying Gourds

Believe it or not, a moldy gourd is actually a good sign. It is a sign that the gourd is drying out and getting ready for future use.

Fresh gourds are about 90 percent water. When they lose that water, they dry with a tough, durable shell. But in the process of drying, your gourds will probably get moldy. If you can stand it, don't throw them away. Instead, handle them gently and put them in a dry, out-of-the-way place like a basement or garage.

If a gourd shrivels, however, you'll need to toss it out, since a shriveled one really has spoiled.

It can take months for a large gourd to dry out. When they are very light and moldy (the seeds may rattle), let them soak for a while in warm water, and you'll find that the outer skin and mold will come off quite easily with an ordinary kitchen scrubbing pad.

Once your gourd has dried, it is ready for whatever you have in mind. Use furniture polish to give it a high shine. Pull out some paints for a creative art project, carve it, wood burn it, anything you like.

Turkey Napkin Ring and Place Card

Combine your napkin ring and place card in one and create a terrific project for the kids.

Construction paper

Marker

Crayons

Pipe cleaners

Glue

Scissors

On a piece of construction paper trace your hand or, better yet, the smaller hands of your children. Cut out one hand for each guest.

Once the handprints are cut out, you simply have to color in your turkey. The palm is the body, the fingers are the feathers, and the thumb is the beak.

Before handing out the turkeys to your kids to decorate, use the marker to print the name of each guest onto the body of the turkey, then let the kids add the beak, eyes and colored feathers.

Once the turkeys are all decorated, take a pipe cleaner and glue the middle of it onto the back of the turkey's body. Once the glue has dried, you can fold the pipe cleaner around your napkin and *voilà!* You have a combination napkin ring and place card.

Cornucopia Place Card

Another attractive place card for the table, and a fun project for kids. With some tasty Bugles (just make sure they don't all get eaten first), construction paper, and dried flowers, you can make these place cards come to life.

Brown or orange construction paper

Bugle corn snacks (enough so that each guest has one)

Small dried flowers—baby's breath works well—or weeds

Marker

Glue

Scissors

Squeeze 2–3 drops of glue inside the Bugle and fill with dried flowers.

While the glue is drying, cut the construction paper into 3- by 4-inch rectangles (about the size of an index card). Fold in half lengthwise and write the name of each guest on the card.

Once the glue has dried, glue each "cornucopia" onto the place card just to the left, right, or underneath the person's name.

Leave flat to dry so the Bugles don't fall off the cards when you set them up.

Centerpieces

For many, finding the perfect centerpiece is almost as hard as cooking the perfect turkey. Of course you could always display a vase of flowers or ring of candles, but what else? Luckily, there is the inspiration of autumn. Just look in your own backyard. Leaves, sticks, and acorns are all used in many of these crafts and ideas. Whatever you do, let your imagination, or those of your children, run wild and enjoy the time to create.

Simple Flowers

Flowers are probably the most common and simplest centerpiece arrangement. When choosing your flowers, consider this top ten list of the most popular seasonal flowers for fall.

1.	Aster	6.	Parrot tulip
2.	Calla lily	7.	Rose
3.	Chocolate cosmos	8.	Statice
4.	Chrysanthemum	9.	Sunflower
5.	Dahlia	10.	Victorian lily

Use a pretty vase and mix and match the flowers however you wish. Or use some of these flowers in the "Autumn Foliage" centerpiece.

Colored Leaf Bouquet

An original take on an old idea. This seasonal bouquet makes a terrific centerpiece or decoration anywhere in the house. Having overnight guests? Why not put one in each room?

Fall leaves, pinecones, bunches of nuts, etc.
Popsicle sticks
Hot glue gun or craft glue
Styrofoam ball or clay
Flower pot
Fall-colored ribbon

Using the hot glue gun or craft glue, attach the leaves, seeds, pinecones, etc., to the ends of Popsicle sticks. To get the best look, you might want to consider attaching one item to each side of the Popsicle stick; this will hide the stick better.

Put the Styrofoam ball or large lump of clay in the bottom of the flower pot and tie the ribbon around the edge of the pot.

Once the glue has dried, stick the ends of the Popsicle sticks into the Styrofoam or clay.

Autumn Foliage

A collection of colorful autumn foliage can be used to create an intimate and inexpensive décor for your table. This centerpiece also provides a fun way for family members of all ages to spend time together.

Gather whatever materials you'd like to have on your table. Let your imagination run away with you and allow children to get creative.

Indian corn
Gourds
Small pumpkins
Acorns
Chestnuts
Leaves
Fir branches

Berries

Chinese lanterns

Dried flowers

You'll also need something to display your foliage on. Consider a flat surface such as a cookie sheet, serving tray, or piece of cardboard.

Other things you'll need are:

Construction paper, fabric, or leftover wallpaper

Glue or tape

Scissors

Ribbons

Pilgrim, Indian, or turkey figurines

Baskets

Start by covering your cookie sheet, tray, or cardboard with paper. If possible, choose colors that will blend well with your foliage. A pastel or neon might be a little overpowering.

Begin assembling the centerpiece by placing one of the larger items in the center of the tray and tucking smaller pieces around it. It's a good idea to rotate the centerpiece as you add items, so it remains interesting to view from all angles.

Once you have an idea of how you would like your centerpiece arranged, you can begin gluing. Start with the larger items and work your way out. This will ensure that a bump on the table won't send the entire arrangement flying.

If you'd like, add ribbon, figurines, or even glitter. Allow your imagination to take over, and most importantly, have fun!

BONUS: Use of a string of cranberries to surround your centerpiece! Take any cranberries left over from your cranberry sauce preparations. Get some thread and a needle and string the cranberries together to form a large circle. Tie off the thread and surround your centerpiece with a fresh string of luscious red cranberries.

A Leafy Table

This attractive table décor is probably the easiest to create and wonderful fun for children and adults alike. At least one week before your Thanksgiving feast, collect, rinse, and pat dry an assortment of colorful autumn leaves.

Once dry, place the leaves between pieces of white tissue paper (make sure the paper is white since colored paper can sometimes bleed) with heavy books on top. Leave them to press for a week in a warm room. This will ensure that the leaves dry flat.

Before setting down the serving dishes, spread the leaves across the table. If you have extra large leaves, you can use them as coasters under stemmed glasses or bowls, or on individual serving plates.

Fall Fruit

A bowl of fall fruit not only makes an attractive centerpiece, but is useful as well. Fill a bowl (a footed compote bowl works best) with apples, pears, nuts, and berries, and not only will your guests admire your handiwork, but dessert is right at hand when the time comes.

Autumnal Offerings

An easy seasonal centerpiece that could also be used on the mantle or other places in the house as decoration.

12-inch glass hurricane shade, a clear glass vase, or glass bowls

Acorns

Pecans

Tiny pumpkins

Fill your container with nuts, fruits, or whatever you find to make an attractive arrangement.

Autumn Wheat Place Settings

Dried herbs or autumn wheat can make the perfect table decoration. Simply wrap a piece of ribbon or a napkin ring around each napkin. When finished, tuck a piece of wheat or small bunch of herbs behind the ring or napkin.

Cornucopia

One of the simplest and most recognizable Thanksgiving centerpieces is the cornucopia, also called horn of plenty. The cornucopia originated in ancient Greece as a symbol for abundance. The original was a curved goat's horn filled to overflowing with fruit and grain. It symbolized the horn possessed by Zeus's nurse, the Greek nymph Amalthaea, which could be filled with whatever the owner wished.

For your own cornucopia you will need a wicker horn, which shouldn't be too hard to find this time of year, and plenty of fruits, nuts, and even cobs of Indian corn. Fill your horn to overflowing and place in the center of the table.

Pumpkin Bowls

These terrific little squash can be used as serving bowls for your cranberry sauce, relish, dips, or even as individual soup bowls. If you are really feeling adventurous, buy a large pumpkin to use not only as a centerpiece, but also as a soup tureen.

You will need:

Miniature pumpkins or squash—as many as desired
Sharp paring knife

Cut the top off each pumpkin and carefully hollow them out. Be sure not to dig too hard or you might puncture the skin of the pumpkin. When finished, fill with your favorite food and place on the table, either with or without the top.

Candles

Next to flowers, candles are one of the simplest and most common centerpieces. It's amazing the way simple candlelight can transform a basic table setting into an intimate affair.

- Line votive candles down the center of a long table for an attractive, low-key decoration.
- Place different-sized taper candles in a direct line down the center of the table, and space them about three inches apart in order of height (put a tall candle in the center with shorter ones going down the line on each side). Or use tapers that are all the same size.
- In the bottom of a wide-topped glass bowl, place nuts, stones, or shells. Fill the bowl with water and add floating candles. If you go to a specialty candle store, you might even be able to find Thanksgiving-theme candles.
- Gather together a collection of natural materials, such as leaves, nuts, or miniature pumpkins, and place them around candelabras or candlesticks.
- Place a single-column candle in a pottery bowl and surround the base of the candle with nuts, leaves, or berries.

When using candles as a centerpiece, be sure to use unscented candles. You would hate to have the scent of your candles overpower the fragrant aromas of your meal.

Gourd Candles

Because gourds come in so many different shapes and sizes, they are natural molds for making your own candles. In addition to lending an organic feel to your table, the gourd candles give us an idea of what it might have been like for the Pilgrims, who had to make candles to provide light.

Squash or gourds (acorn squash works well)

Beeswax (1 pound for a 2-pound squash)

Paring knife

6-inch chef's knife

Spoon

Pencil or chopstick

Aniline dyes

Wicks and wick tabs

Tin cans or aluminum foil

Candy thermometer

Wicks come in a broad range of sizes and styles. Choosing the right wick is important and can impact the success of your candle. Wicks are usually classified by diameter. The larger the diameter of the candle, the larger the wick you will need. Square-braided wicks are the best choice for beeswax candles, pillars, and blocks.

Cut off the top of the gourd with a paring knife, making the opening large enough so that you can remove the seeds and pulp. Using the spoon, scoop out the seeds and flesh, being careful not to cut into the skin of the gourd.

Once most of the pulp has been cleaned out, carefully scrape around the inside of the skin, following the contours of the gourd. If you have a gourd or small pumpkin that is ridged, make sure the ridges are defined on the inside so that they will shape your candle in the same way. Make sure the interior of the squash is clear and well defined.

Using a double boiler, melt the wax to a temperature of 180 degrees F (check temperature with a candy thermometer). It takes about 20 minutes to melt a 1-pound block of wax.

As the wax melts, add the dye. Aniline dyes are very concentrated, so all you need is a small chip. Allow the dye to melt into the wax.

While the wax is heating, cut a piece of wicking 3 inches longer than the height of the squash. Attach a metal wick tab to one end. Crimp the tab shut using pliers.

Prime the wick by dipping it into the wax for 60 seconds. You will see air bubbles exiting the braid. Keep the wick submerged in the wax until there are no more air bubbles. Remove the wick, and hold it taut until it cools.

Set the squash in a tin can, or make a "nest" out of foil, to steady it as you work. Pour the melted wax into the squash, just below the top. Pour slowly to avoid creating air bubbles. Be careful not to drip any water or condensation into the wax.

Once the gourd has been filled, carefully drop the wick into the wax at the squash's center (it will sink to the bottom). Place the pencil across the top of the gourd, and wrap or tie the wick around the pencil.

Let the gourd sit until it is cool to the touch, 4 to 5 hours. (If the center of the candle sinks during cooling, you can add more hot wax.)

When the gourd is cool, peel away the skin. It may be necessary to score the surface with a utility knife. The skin of the gourd should break away easily, leaving a uniquely formed candle.

If your candle doesn't sit flat, you can smooth out the bottom by rubbing it against a flat heated surface to melt and flatten it slightly. An old pie tin set briefly atop a double boiler will do the trick. Place the candle on the heated tin, and simply move it in a circular motion. Cool on wax paper.

Candle Apples

❖❖

Place these floating candles in a crystal bowl filled with water for a terrific centerpiece, or use them as an outdoor decoration by evoking memories of bobbing for apples. Simply fill a galvanized tub with water and drop in as many candles as it can hold. What a great way to greet people at your front door!

Apples
Votive candles
Paring knife

Since every apple floats and sits differently, you should start by testing out the way they float. Drop each apple into a sink or bowl filled with water. When you see how it floats, make a mark to show where the candle should sit without tilting.

With a paring knife, carefully cut a hole in the apple as deep as the votive is tall, and as wide as the candle is wide. In other words, the candle should sit snugly in the hole and just so the top of the candle is even with the top of the apple.

You might want to draw the circle on the apple, cut it into sections, and spoon it out with a melon baller or teaspoon.

Squeeze lemon juice into the cut to keep the apple from turning brown, and insert a votive candle.

Candle Tips

To keep candles burning longer, store them in the refrigerator and set them out just before lighting.

Coat the candles with vegetable spray to make the wax easier to remove, if it should drip on candleholders or the tablecloth.

If wax drips on silver candlesticks, put them in the freezer for an hour. The wax will peel off easily without damaging the silver.

Peter Peter Pumpkin Light

These adorable pumpkin lights make not only great centerpieces, but terrific outdoor decorations as well. After all, who says you can carve pumpkins only at Halloween?

> Small pumpkins (not miniature, though, they won't carve well)
> Carving or paring knife
> Spoon
> Candles

Cut the tops off the pumpkins just as you would a pumpkin at Halloween and scoop out all the insides, being careful not to poke a hole through the skin.

Unlike a jack-o'-lantern, your Thanksgiving pumpkin should be carved all the way around so everyone at the table can enjoy it. Poke holes, make triangles, or even create patterns on paper and trace onto your pumpkin.

Candle Etiquette

When using taper candles as centerpieces, make sure they are at least two inches below the eye level of your guests. Forcing your guests to gaze through or around a candle flame is irritating to everyone.

Light the candles just before the guests are seated, and allow them to burn until the meal is finished, unless of course you see them burning too low.

The proper way to extinguish candles is by using a candlesnuffer. Snuffers also cut down on the danger of flying wax.

Decorating Outside

As the Thanksgiving host or hostess you know you're going to work hard to decorate the inside of your home, and especially your table, but why not go the extra mile and greet guests with special decorations the minute they pull in the driveway? Some of these simple, yet attractive ideas will put everyone in the holiday spirit before they even get out of the car.

Window Boxes

Even in the warmest climates, it's pretty rare that your window boxes are looking all that good around Thanksgiving. Well, you can fix that with ease. Replace all your dying or dead flowers and plants with gourds, pumpkins, and Indian corn. Not only will you have a seasonal decoration, but your neighbors will be impressed with your ingenuity.

Mums

Mums are the quintessential flower of fall. Easy to come by and inexpensive, these terrific flowers can easily brighten up your home's entrance. Add a few pots of mums to your doorstep or along the walkway.

Fall Wreath

Who says that Christmas is the only holiday for a wreath? This great wreath can hang on your door throughout the fall and be packed away for use next year.

> Fall leaves, pinecones, nuts, etc.
> Cardboard
> Hot glue gun
> Large bow in fall-colored ribbon
> Fall-colored ribbons

After collecting your leaves, pinecones, etc., let them sit out for a day or two to allow them to dry.

Cut a large circle, oval, or square (whatever shape or size you choose) out of the cardboard. Use the hot glue gun to attach the leaves, seeds, etc., to the wreath, and the large bow.

Use the other ribbon to hang the wreath from, or to hang nuts or pinecones in the center of the wreath.

Pinecone Wreath

By just interchanging the ribbon, this festive wreath can easily be used at Christmas too.

> Grapevine wreath
> Pinecones
> Hot glue gun
> Wired-edged ribbon

Hot glue the pinecones to the wreath (use plenty of glue since the pinecones are heavy). You can glue as many or as few as you want. Use them as accents to the grapevine, or cover the grapevine completely so it looks as if your entire wreath is made of pinecones.

Let the wreath dry overnight.

Use the wired ribbon to decorate the wreath. Weave it around the pinecones, or make a big bow.

Decorating Inside

Once you've decided on a centerpiece and determined how long the turkey needs to cook, it's time to take a close look at the rest of your house. Wouldn't your guests be thrilled by a fall mobile in the bathroom or herb garland around the fireplace? Remember, Thanksgiving is an autumn holiday and many of these ideas can look festive well before this November day.

Herb Garland

Gather together bunches of dried herbs and flowers. With a string, tie them all together so the bunches overlap the stems of the previous flower.

When finished, the garland can be draped either on the table, along the wall, or on the mantel.

Fall Mobile

A great decoration for Thanksgiving and a great craft for the kids.

At least one week before Thanksgiving, collect, rinse, and pat dry an assortment of colorful autumn leaves. Make sure you get leaves of many different colors, sizes, and shapes.

Once dry, place the leaves between pieces of white tissue paper (make sure the paper is white, since colored paper can sometimes bleed) with heavy books on top. Leave to press for a week in a warm room. This will ensure that the leaves dry flat.

Find three sticks of varying size and weight. The largest and heaviest stick will be the top support of your mobile.

With string or thread, hang the thinner sticks off the end of the top stick. Try to make them different heights and at a size that they balance evenly.

Once you have the sticks hanging, attach the leaves in whatever order or pattern you desire. Try to balance them by weight so the mobile hangs straight.

Favorite Tables

So often people work hard to make the perfect table decoration, love it, and then forget what they did the year before. Secure your memories by taking note of them here.

Decoration Name _____ Year _____

Insert Photograph

What I did to create this table:

Decoration Name ———— Year ————

Insert Photograph

What I did to create this table:

Decoration Name _____ Year _____

Insert Photograph

What I did to create this table:

Decoration Name _____ Year _____

Insert Photograph

What I did to create this table:

Decoration Name ———————————— Year ———

Insert Photograph

What I did to create this table:

5

Turkey Day Trivia

Now what I want is, Facts . . .
Facts alone are wanted in life.
—Charles Dickens

From the Macy's Thanksgiving Day Parade to Thomas Jefferson's love of the turkey, the facts and trivia surrounding Thanksgiving are fun and far-reaching. Use this chapter as a competitive trivia game among family members or just as a way to stimulate conversation during dinner. By the way, do you know what the longest balloon in the Macy's Thanksgiving Day Parade is?

Thanksgiving Feast

Benjamin Franklin was very disappointed when the bald eagle was chosen as the national symbol of our country. In fact, he said, "I wish the Bald Eagle had not been chosen as the representative of our country: he is a Bird of bad moral character: like those among Men who live by Sharping and Robbing, he is generally poor and very often lousy. The Turkey is a much more respectable Bird and withal a true original Native of North America."

If Franklin had gotten his way, we might be eating bald eagle instead of turkey at Thanksgiving.

The Native Americans' (whom the Pilgrims called Indians) word for corn was *maize*.

Along with deer and vegetables, the Indians brought popcorn to the first Thanksgiving.

When the pilgrims first came to this country, they learned from the Indians that the cranberry, or *ibimi* in Wampanoas, was good for a lot more than just sauce. The cranberry is a small, sour berry that grows in bogs. The Indians used the fruit to treat infections and dye cloth.

The top five most popular ways to serve leftover Thanksgiving turkey are:

1. Sandwich
2. Soup or stew
3. Casserole
4. Stir-fry
5. Salad

Before being harvested and sold, an individual cranberry must bounce at least four inches high to make sure they are not too ripe!

Male turkeys are called toms, female turkeys are called hens, and baby turkeys are called poults.

Toms (male turkeys) reach market weight—about 24 pounds—approximately 19 to 20 weeks after they hatch.

The heaviest turkey ever recorded was the 75-pound turkey raised by a turkey farming company in 1967.

The first meal eaten on the moon by astronauts Neil Armstrong and Buzz Aldrin was roasted turkey and all the trimmings!

The tradition of breaking the wishbone was believed to have started in 322 B.C. with hens, not turkeys. At the time it was believed that hens could tell the future.

In 1999 U.S. farmers produced 273 million turkeys, which weighed a total of 6.9 billion pounds.

North Carolina and Minnesota are the nation's two leading turkey-producing states.

Wisconsin, Massachusetts, and New Jersey lead the nation in cranberry production.

In 1999 U.S. farmers produced 639 million pounds of cranberries.

In 1999 U.S. farmers also produced 599,000 tons of sweet potatoes.

North Carolina, Louisiana, and California are leading states in sweet potato production.

When the Air Force was first conducting test runs on breaking the sound barrier, fields of turkeys would drop dead from apparent heart attacks.

Turkeys can drown if they look up when it is raining.

❊

A frightened turkey can run at speeds up to 20 miles per hour. If really threatened, they can leap into flight, approaching speeds between 50 and 55 mph in a matter of seconds.

❊

Because the Pilgrims didn't have domesticated cattle, they didn't have any milk or butter to make pumpkin pie. So while most Americans think it is a crucial ending to their meal, it wasn't part of the original Thanksgiving feast. Instead, they ate boiled pumpkin.

❊

The United States turkey industry produces a total income of about $1 billion a year.

❊

Each person in the United States consumes an average of 18 pounds of turkey each year.

Thanksgiving History

Women and some indentured servants were prohibited from signing the Mayflower Compact.

In 1827 Sarah Josepha Hale, editor of *Godey's Lady's Book*, a magazine for women, started writing articles about Thanksgiving. She told stories about the Pilgrims and their harvest celebration and wrote editorials suggesting a national holiday. For thirty-six years Ms. Hale fought for Thanksgiving Day, but without success. It wasn't until 1863, when she sent a personal letter to Secretary of State William Seward, that she finally received attention. Secretary of State Seward like the idea so much that he showed it to President Lincoln, and this spurred Lincoln to proclaim the last Thursday in November Thanksgiving Day, making it a national holiday.

Shortly after President George Washington's Thanksgiving Proclamation was written in 1778, it was lost for over a hundred years. Apparently the document was misplaced or attached to some private papers in the process of moving official records from one city to another when the capital was changed. The original manuscript did not appear in the official presidential archives until 1921, when Dr. J. C. Fitzpatrick, then assistant chief of the manuscripts division of the Library of Congress, "found" the proclamation. It was at an auction sale being held at an art gallery in New York. It was written in longhand by William Jackson, secretary to President Washington, and was signed by George Washington. Dr. Fitzpatrick purchased the document for $300 for the Library of Congress, where it now resides.

The *Mayflower* was estimated to have measured 113 feet long from the back rail to the end of the bow.

✳

Contrary to popular perception, Pilgrims did not have buckles on their clothing, shoes, or hats.

Because the Pilgrims said they were heading for "Northern Virginia," it is often assumed that they were off course by about 500 miles. This, in fact, is not true. The Pilgrims were headed to an area owned by the Virginia Company which had rights to almost the entire Eastern seaboard of America. "Northern Virginia" actually refers to the region that would be roughly southern New York State. Based on current knowledge, it is clear that the Pilgrims originally intended to settle the Hudson River region in New York.

It was hard work being a Pilgrim child in 1600s New England. Chores often included: fetching water from the brook, gathering firewood, herding animals, gathering berries and other wild plants, and helping their parents cook, clean, preserve food, plant and harvest crops, and care for younger children.

Pilgrim children were expected to bow or curtsy to all adults, including their parents. Both Pilgrim boys and girls wore gowns or dresses until they were about seven years old.

Since bathing was considered unhealthy, most Pilgrims probably took baths only a few times a year.

Thanksgiving Today

Franklin D. Roosevelt tried to move Thanksgiving ahead by one week to the third week in November to create a longer Christmas shopping season and to reduce government expenses. Unfortunately, there was such a public uproar that it was restored to the fourth week the following year.

It is estimated that more that 32 million people travel between the Wednesday and Sunday of Thanksgiving weekend.

The busiest travel day of the year is the Friday after Thanksgiving, when you can expect that almost 14 million people are on the move.

There are three towns in the U.S. named after the star of the Thanksgiving feast—Turkey, Texas (pop. 442), Turkey Creek, Louisiana (pop. 305), and Turkey, North Carolina (pop. 286).

The first Thanksgiving Day pro football game was played in 1934 between the Detroit Lions and the Chicago Bears as a way to boost the popularity of the newly formed Detroit Lions. Although the Lions lost 19–16, the game was a success, with all 26,000 seats selling out two weeks before the event.

In this 1962 film, *The Man Who Shot Liberty Valance*, John Wayne always called Jimmy Stewart's character "Pilgrim." From then on, the phrase has long been associated with "The Duke" (as John Wayne was called).

In the popular Thanksgiving television special, *A Charlie Brown Thanksgiving*, Chef Snoopy strays from the traditional to serve the gang popcorn and toast.

Twenty-five passengers on the *Mayflower* have descendants who are still living today.

The following presidents are all said to be descendents of *Mayflower* passengers: John Adams, John Quincy Adams, Zachary Taylor, Ulysses S. Grant, James A. Garfield, Franklin D. Roosevelt, George H.W. Bush, and George W. Bush.

Macy's Thanksgiving Day Parade

Over 60 million people each year watch the Macy's Thanksgiving Day Parade on television.

At 78 feet, Spider-Man is the longest balloon ever featured at the Macy's Parade.

The Macy's Thanksgiving Day Parade first occurred in 1924 and was canceled only once, between the years 1942 and 1944 so that the rubber from the balloons could be donated to the war effort.

In 1957, Popeye's cap collected so much water that he would periodically careen off balance, dumping gallons of water on spectators.

A helium shortage in 1958 meant that ballon operators and Macy's officials needed to get inventive. Since the parade must go on, the balloons were filled with air and directed down the parade route while dangling from cranes.

Felix the Cat was the first balloon character to appear in the Macy's Thanksgiving Day Parade. He took flight for the first time in 1927. Before that, the parade consisted of floats, zoo animals, and Macy's employees, and any balloons used were released and would float for days.

Garfield has the record for the most appearances in the Macy's Thanksgiving Day Parade. This well-fed balloon appeared in his sixteenth parade in 1999.

6

Family Fun and Traditions of Thanks

How wonderful it would be if we could help our children and grandchildren to learn thanksgiving at an early age. Thanksgiving opens the doors. It changes a child's personality. A child is resentful, negative—or thankful. Thankful children want to give, they radiate happiness, they draw people.

—Sir John Templeton

Thanksgiving is a holiday when most of the traditions center on what you will be eating. However, for many people it is the one time of year when the entire family is able to gather together. If that's the case, it might be a good time to think of some special traditions your family can start or create for Thanksgiving.

Giving Thanks

Once the blessing has been said and everyone has food on their plate, there is no better way to share a Thanksgiving than for each person to take a turn expressing all those things they are thankful for.

Remember, the Pilgrims first celebrated Thanksgiving as a way to give thanks to God for the bountiful harvest they were blessed with that year. Continue this tradition by going around the table and asking everyone to share in their own bountiful harvest. This is a tradition that even the littlest child can share in. Whether you are thankful for your health, your family, your new job, or that it's not raining, giving thanks is a delightful way for everyone to realize their blessings.

As host or hostess, you might want to start. That way everyone will have an understanding of the game. Start by saying, "I'm thankful for . . ." and name one or two things that you are truly thankful for.

An Alphabet of Thanks

For a variation on the idea of giving thanks, why not make it easier by asking everyone to give thanks from A to Z. Start with the eldest guest, or the person seated at the head of the table. This person begins by saying they are thankful for something that starts with the letter "A," the next person, "B," the next, "C," and so on.

For a real brain teaser, you can require each person to repeat what everyone else has said. For instance, "I'm thankful for eggplant, Aunt Becky is thankful for dogs, Grandma Lila is thankful for chocolate, Dad is thankful for bread, and Christopher is thankful for the apple pie."

Being Glad

In the book *Pollyanna* by Eleanor H. Porter, and later the movie starring Hayley Mills, Pollyanna is the relentlessly optimist little orphan who is forced to live with her dour and unhappy aunt. If anyone had mastery over Being Glad, it was Pollyanna.

One Christmas, Pollyanna breaks both her legs and says,

"I'm so glad, glad, glad it happened! For you have to lose your legs to really love them!" And that's where Being Glad comes in.

To play Being Glad, think of something really awful that happened to you in the past year, and then tell everyone at the Thanksgiving table why you're grateful for it. For example, you might start the game by saying, "I'm so very glad that our electricity went out. If it hadn't have happened, I wouldn't have learned to appreciate all the great things I can do without TV or radio."

The Talking Fork

This old storytelling game is a variation on the "Talking Stick," an ancient human storytelling tradition. In Homer's *Iliad*, warrior kings would pass the ribboned staff around the room. The holder of the staff was the one whose turn it was to speak. Likewise, Native Americans still pass the Talking Stick from storyteller to storyteller.

In this game, we will use a fork instead of a stick. Since this is Thanksgiving, the holiday of eating, the fork is a most appropriate symbol. Choose a large serving fork for dramatic effect and tie a pretty bow or ribbon around it.

Start the game by saying, "This fork, although it appears ordinary, gives the user storyteller power. While you hold this fork, memories of Thanksgivings past will flow through you. While you hold this fork, everyone will listen.

"Before we all leave, I want to hear some good, fun, magical family stories. Since I hold the Talking Fork, I'll go first."

This is an especially terrific game for families who are scattered all over the country and aren't able to get together much. The Talking Fork allows everyone to learn a little bit of family history. Encourage Mom, Dad, aunts, uncles, and grandparents to share stories from their childhood or about someone special who is no longer with you.

Regale the family with tales of the quirks, funny sayings, or adventures of your beloved ancestors. Or you can tell stories about your own children. How they behaved as tempestuous toddlers and the origins of their pet names. Or maybe what happened the day they were born.

Recording the Fork

If you have a video camera or tape recorder, the Talking Fork is the perfect time to turn that equipment on. These are stories and moments that will last forever and you'll appreciate having them on tape in years to come.

Sharing the Thanks

After reading all about what the Pilgrims had to endure those first years in America and then sharing all the wonderful things you and your family have to be thankful for, it is only fair that you feel compelled to share your wealth.

While volunteering during the holidays and especially during Thanksgiving is common, there are still a surprising number of people and organizations that need help. Whether you decide to spend the day at a soup kitchen or helping in your church, volunteering on Thanksgiving should be something the entire family can do together.

If you are volunteering, ask organizers if there is something special they would like younger children to do. If not, plan an activity that makes your children feel needed. Have them decorate the hall or help clear dishes. If you plan on putting together a Thanksgiving basket, include your children in putting together the items and even choosing some of the food or clothes you donate.

Whatever you decide, there are many people and organizations who appreciate any help they can get. Here are just a few suggestions for getting the entire family involved. If none of these interest you, contact your church or a local community group to see where you can assist.

- Call a local church or soup kitchen and volunteer to work on Thanksgiving Day. Many places even have jobs for children.
- Contact a nursing home or senior center to see if any seniors would like to spend the day with your family.

- Invite a family from a battered women's shelter or homeless shelter to share in your meal.
- Ask all your guests to bring old clothing or cans of food that you can donate to a local homeless shelter or church.
- Prepare a Thanksgiving basket with a fully cooked meal consisting of turkey, stuffing, mashed potatoes, and cranberry sauce. Give the basket to a social service agency or civic group, who can then deliver it to a family that would otherwise have nothing to eat.
- Contact a local church or synagogue to find out if they know of any families in need. Either put together a Thanksgiving basket or buy a gift certificate from your supermarket to present to the family.
- Look into your local meals-on-wheels organization or contact your church to find out if any families or individuals in your area are homebound. If so, volunteer to deliver a hot meal to them. Bring the kids and enjoy Thanksgiving dinner together.

Thanksgiving Touch Football

Football and Thanksgiving go hand in hand, so why not move from the couch to the playing field. Not only is touch football a great way to burn off some of those extra Thanksgiving calories, but it will also get everyone out of the house for some fresh air and family bonding. Whether you choose to play before or after dinner (we recommend before to avoid any upset stomachs), follow these rules to ensure that everyone is on the same wavelength.

Before beginning play, there are a number of things you will need to decide. First, choose a grassy area to serve as your playing field (look for something not too close to a road in case your quarterback is a little wild). Set your playing field's boundaries and use brightly colored bandannas or rags to mark them. If you have cones, even better. The playing field should be rectangular, with an end zone at each end. Anything outside the playing area is out of bounds.

Divide players evenly into two teams. When playing with family members of all ages, try to make sure that the ages are evenly distributed between the teams. Rather than choosing captains, which often ends in hurt feelings when someone is chosen last, why not plan the teams ahead of time and just hand out the rosters?

Give each team a few minutes to decide who will act as quarterback, running backs, receivers, and line players. You might want to mix things up a bit and have people take turns in various positions. You might be surprised to find out that your six-year-old is actually the best quarterback or that Grandma makes a terrific lineman.

Discuss between the two teams whether you'll play one-hand touch or two-hand touch. This will determine whether or not you need to "tackle" the ballcarrier by tagging her with one or two hands. Two-handed touch tends to be a little more difficult and may make for a longer game. If you have a number of younger children, you will probably want to play one-handed.

Decide how a winner will be determined. The best ways are either by limiting playing time or choosing a score. For example, the winning team could be the one with the higher score at the end of an hour or the first team to score 21 points.

Make a decision about whether you want to earn new first downs. In traditional football, teams have four tries, or downs, to gain at least 10 yards. If they do so, they start over with a new set of downs. Downs might be difficult for you to play. For one thing, you would need to determine and measure out what 10 yards would be. Another problem is that your field might not be big enough. The rules that follow describe a game without first downs.

And last but not least in your game preparation, flip a coin to decide which team will begin playing offense.

To play the game, begin by placing the ball in the middle of the field.

Each team should gather in separate huddles to discuss strategy. Once strategies have been decided, line up the teams on either side of the ball, parallel to the end zones and facing each other.

The offensive player in the center of the line (the "center") passes the ball to the quarterback between his legs. If you don't have enough players, you can eliminate the "center" and allow the quarterback to handle the ball himself.

While the "offensive linemen" block the defensive line, the quarterback hands off the ball to a running back or passes the ball to a receiver, who then runs with the ball toward the opposite end zone while defensive players try to tag him or her.

Other offensive players try to keep defenders from tagging the ball carrier by blocking for him or her.

Once the player has been tagged, play stops and the ball is dropped where the tag was made. This counts as a down and play is repeated. Downs are also ended when a ball is dropped or a player runs out of bounds.

Once four downs have been completed, possession of the ball is switched and the defense then becomes the offense at the point where the ball was last in play. The new offense gets four attempts to move the ball toward the opposite end zone.

If a team scores, earning them 7 points, possession of the ball is also switched. After a touchdown is made, play begins again by setting the ball in the middle of the field and lining the teams up as before.

Continue playing until the point or time limit is reached.

The Thanksgiving Family Pool

If you are like most Americans, the minute dinner winds down and the dishes are done, it is time to flip on the TV and enjoy a rousing game of football. Whether you settle in front of the game to cheer on your favorite team, or just to catch a few winks, it seems there are few households who miss the traditional Cowboys or Lions game. To make the game more exciting for fans and nonfans alike, why not set up a betting pool to include everyone in on the competition?

For those who don't like the idea of betting with money, here are a few options that follow the betting idea but in a more wholesome (and legal) manner:

- Allow the winner or top winners to opt out of cleanup (if it hasn't already been done).
- Make up a grab bag of gifts and allow people to choose according to their place in the pool.

- Ask everyone to pitch in money and the winner, instead of keeping the cash, gets to donate it to his or her favorite charity.
- Instead of cash, ask everyone to bring a white elephant gift to bet with. The winner gets to take all the gifts home. You might find people trying to lose this one!

The betting game proposed below is perfect for everyone. You don't need to have any knowledge of football to play, or win. You just need to have a little luck.

Begin your pool by drawing a 10-by-10 grid on a piece of paper (10 squares on top, 10 on the side). Across the top and down the left side write the numbers 0–9 (as shown in the figure).

Above the numbers, along the top of the grid, write the name of one of the teams playing (Dallas Cowboys) and write the name of the other team along the side (Detroit Lions).

Once your grid has been established, you can begin "selling" squares. Sell them for as little or as much as you want. One square for a penny, nickel, or dollar, or ten squares for a gag gift. Or feel free to give them out. Maybe each guest gets five squares. However you do it, it's best to try to have each square filled before the game starts.

When a "buyer" takes a square, write her initials in the box.

When the game is over (for those who actually watch), the winner is determined by matching the last digit of each team's final score with the grid. For example, a score of Dallas 13, Detroit 26 would mean finding the square where 3 on the vertical scale meets 6 on the horizontal. If Sally chose the space where these two numbers meet, she's the winner.

More Family Fun: Games

Charades

Charades is a terrific family game for kids of all ages. While it started out as a riddle game where you guessed a word, it eventually evolved into the acting game we know today. It can be played with four or more players, two (or more) teams.

What you will need:

- A 3-minute timer
- Pen and paper to keep score and paper to write your charade words on
- A neutral player to keep time and score

The objective of Charades is for players to act out a word, an idea, the name of a person, movie, book, song, or television show in the shortest amount of time possible.

Pick some categories that will be fun to guess. Write the titles on small scraps of paper and throw them into a hat for the other team to pull out. The first team pulls a scrap of paper from the collection of titles the other team has created. A team member has to act out the title without speaking. Team members guess until they answer the puzzle correctly. When the answer is guessed the timer stops. When a player guesses part of the answer correctly, point to the player and nod enthusiastically. One point is scored per correct answer per team. Team with the most points wins! When time is up you are out—even if no points were scored!

Here are some helpful hand movements for helping your teammates figure out what the heck you are doing!

A movie: pretend you are cranking a projector

A television show: make a box in the air in front of your body with your hands

A book: hold open your hands, palms up, as if you are cradling a book

Quote or phrase: Make quotation marks in the air with your fingers

Song: Pretend you are singing: Open your mouth wide!

Length of word: Make a "little" or "big" sign using your hands (A "little" sign can be made by using your thumb and index finger, a "big" sign can be made by holding both hands apart as if measuring a fish.)

First word, second word, etc.: Hold up your finger to show which word you are acting out

Numbers: show on fingers

Sounds like: pull ear lobe

Number of syllables: hold up fingers to show number and then tap fingers on opposite outstretched arm

Hide and Seek

What memories a good game of Hide and Seek can bring back for the older folks. This family favorite can bring out the child in all of us. No materials are necessary to play a good game, just a great imagination.

The object of the game is for several people to hide and for one person to seek the hiders. To play the game, choose someone to be "It." To pick that person, put everyone's name in a hat and pull one out. The person whose name is pulled has to be "It" first. Pick a home base. This is the place from which the "It" person will count and the place to which all players want to return. Each player will hide, then try to get back to home base without being tagged by the "It" person. The first person tagged is "It" in the next game, but whoever is "It" should try to find all players before the game is over.

If you are "It," close your eyes and count to 50 while everyone else finds a good place to hide. Count loudly so each person knows how much time is left. When you reach 50, yell out: "Ready or not, here I come!" Let the games begin!

Telephone

The more players you have for Telephone, the better, but don't play with less than six players or it probably won't work very well. The objective is to deliver a message correctly to all players in the game. You'd be surprised how different the original message is from the message the last player gets, and the younger the kids, the funner the game!

Players should sit in a circle. One player is the message giver and whispers the message he invents to the player on his right. The message may not be written down or repeated. This player in turn whispers the message into the ear of the next person to his right. The play continues around the circle until the last player delivers the message to the person who started the game. When it has come full circle, the first person recites the message he just received from the last player. You may be very surprised at the outcome! Imagine what happens to a story that travels around a whole school!

Word Games

Anagrams

Anagrams can be played with everyone: There is no limit to the number of players you can have. Here's how to play:

Each player should have his own piece of paper and pen or pencil. Have an egg timer handy.

Pick a word that has a lot of letters in it. Each player should write the word down on his own sheet of paper. Turn over the timer and let the fun begin. Each player must make as many words from the original word as he can. You can change the rules to suit the age group. Younger children can have shorter words, while older children should try to make words of four letters or more (you can adjust scoring to be fair to younger players). When the timer is finished the game is over. Pick one player to read out the words he wrote down. If any other player has that word, each player who has it crosses it off his list. You only score points if you come up with words that no one else has on their list.

<u>Scoring</u>

Each 2-letter word equals one point.
Each 3-letter word equals two points.
Each 4-letter word equals three points and so on.

Pick a point value to play up to and the first person to reach it wins!

Alphabets

Alphabets is another fun word game. As with anagrams, all you need is a pen and a piece of paper for each team member, and an egg timer. Any number of people can play.

Find ten categories that will be fun to play with. Here are some fun ones to try:

- Flower
- Name of a girl
- Name of a boy
- Book title
- Author
- Actor
- Actress
- Car
- Tree
- Color
- Gemstone
- State
- Country
- Capital
- Politician
- Relative
- Weather
- Body of water
- Mountain

Each player should write down the chosen categories on his piece of paper, one category per line. Have a player pick a letter from the alphabet and have each player write the letter at the top of the list. Turn the egg timer over and have each player try to fill in each category with a word beginning with the chosen letter. When the time is up, one player can read his words aloud. Each player who has the same word will cross it off the list. One point is scored for each word no one else has.

For example, if the letter is B, you could do the following:

Flower: buttercup
Name of a boy: Brian
Name of a girl: Betty
Country: Bosnia
Body of water: Baltic Sea
Weather: breezy

And so on! If you write down two words using the letter you get two points. For example: Relative: big brother.

2 points!

Sentence by Sentence

The object of Sentence by Sentence is to build a complete story by adding a sentence to a series of sentences. The catch is that only the previous sentence is known to you. The results are often very silly and get kids of all ages giggling up a storm.

All you need is a piece of paper and someone to write down a sentence as if he was starting a story. For example, the first person writes down:

It was nighttime when suddenly the lights went out.

The next player receives the paper from the first player and adds a sentence on the line right below the first sentence. Before giving the paper to the next player, however, he must cover the first sentence by folding the paper over so only the second sentence is now visible.

First player: *It was nighttime when suddenly the lights went out.*

Second player: *Bob knew that meant the food in the fridge wouldn't last long.*

Now the third player only sees the second player's sentence, so he adds a sentence based on that.

Third player: *With Aunt Mabel in the house, there was never enough food left for everyone else.*

And so on. No matter how your story ends up, it gets those brains whirring and the imagination flying. Always a good game for some family laughs.

A Family of Friends

So often Thanksgiving is thought of as a holiday spent with family. However, these days it seems that a Thanksgiving with family is getting harder to do. With families spread out all over the country, and sometimes the world, not everyone is able to make it home for the holiday.

If you're someone with family or friends who live far away, you might want to consider gathering a group of "strays" to enjoy the holiday. Throw the party at your house, offering to make the turkey, and ask everyone to bring a dish to pass. Either a bowl of cranberries, an apple pie, or just a can of green beans. Whatever your guests have to offer, we can guarantee that a Thanksgiving with a group is a lot better than sitting home and eating popcorn in front of the football game.

For those with both friends and family scattered across the country, holidays and vacations can be a time of stress. Often family asks you to go one way, while friends beg you to go another.

We know of a group of friends who have tried to remedy this problem by making Thanksgiving their own special holiday. With the blessings of their families, they have spent the last five years of Thanksgivings traveling to one home or another for quality friend time and a delicious vegetarian Thanksgiving meal.

No matter how busy their year gets and how hard it might be to get together, this small group knows that at least around Thanksgiving they will have a chance to enjoy a good meal and reconnect with one another.

Thanksgiving Memory Book

If Thanksgiving is the one time of year you are able to gather your family, or your friends, then it is also the perfect time for a special family photo.

Make an event of the family photo each year by gathering everyone together in either the same spot or at the same time. Maybe you'll want to pose after the touch football game or around the Thanksgiving table. Whatever you do, gather the pictures each year in a special Thanksgiving memory album. Or include them in the pages at the back of this book.

What fun it will be to bring out the album each year to see how the kids have grown or to count the new additions!

When putting the album together, add quotes or fun stories of the day. You could even include a list of what everyone was thankful for. It might be fun to look back ten years from now to see what everyone said.

The Meaning of Thanksgiving

Many countries throughout the world have a harvest festival of some kind. In North America, Thanksgiving is the most common autumn celebration, but what does it really mean, and how should you explain it to your children?

1. Explain the ancient origins of the harvest festival to your children. In ancient times, people of many cultures (including the ancient Greeks, Romans, Hebrews, Egyptians, and Chinese) gave thanks to their god or gods for a successful harvest, and some of the traditions associated with modern Thanksgiving celebrations have their roots in these ancient festivals.

2. Discuss the roots of the American Thanksgiving celebration. In 1621, near the end of the Plymouth Colony's first year in America, the settlers gave thanks for a plentiful first harvest. The Pilgrims and the natives celebrated together, and everyone feasted on geese, ducks, deer, corn, oysters, fish, and berries.

3. Discuss Native American issues surrounding Thanksgiving. Despite the harmonious relations that may have existed between natives and Pilgrims at the first Thanksgiving feast, many subsequent American Thanksgivings involved settlers giving thanks for victories over the natives. Ask your children how they feel about this, and discuss the recent efforts that have been made by the American government and people to apologize for past discrimination and violence.

4. Explain when—and why—Thanksgiving became an official holiday. In 1863, during the Civil War, President Abraham Lincoln proclaimed that Thanksgiving should be a national observance. To some degree, this was a way to brighten the spirits of the American people, who were dealing with a great deal of difficulty and deprivation.

5. Explain that one aspect of Thanksgiving involves gratitude for having enough food to eat, and encourage your children to help you buy groceries for the food bank, or make a donation to a local soup kitchen.

6. Talk turkey. The wild turkey is native to the Eastern states and northern Mexico, and while it probably wasn't served at the first Thanksgiving feast, it has become a symbol of the holiday.

7. Offer your children some relevant books. Many books that discuss the Thanksgiving tradition from a variety of different perspectives are available for readers of all ages.

Let your children help with preparations for your Thanksgiving meal, and encourage them to make appropriate decorations. This gives you an opportunity to discuss the symbolism of many objects associated with Thanksgiving, and to share family traditions with them as you prepare the feast together.

Our Family Traditions and Memories

Whether you have special traditions of your own you'd like to write down, or Thanksgiving memories you'd like to share with generations to come, this is a great spot to fill those ideas in and record them forever.

TRADITION/MEMORY _____

RECORDER _____

_____

_____

_____

_____

_____

_____

_____

_____

_____

_____

_____

_____

_____

TRADITION/MEMORY _____

RECORDER _____

_____
_____
_____
_____
_____
_____
_____
_____
_____
_____
_____
_____
_____
_____
_____

❖❖

TRADITION/MEMORY _____

RECORDER _____

_____
_____
_____
_____
_____
_____
_____
_____
_____
_____
_____
_____
_____
_____

TRADITION/MEMORY _____

RECORDER _____

_____
_____
_____
_____
_____
_____
_____
_____
_____
_____
_____
_____
_____
_____

❖❖

TRADITION/MEMORY _____

RECORDER _____

_____
_____
_____
_____
_____
_____
_____
_____
_____
_____
_____
_____
_____
_____
_____

TRADITION/MEMORY _____

RECORDER _____

_____

_____

_____

_____

_____

_____

_____

_____

_____

_____

_____

_____

❖❖

TRADITION/MEMORY _____

RECORDER _____

_____

_____

_____

_____

_____

_____

_____

_____

_____

_____

_____

_____

_____

_____

7

Thanksgiving Around the World

It is the duty of all Nations to acknowledge the
providence of Almighty God,
to obey his will, to be grateful for his benefits,
and humbly to implore his protection and favor.

—George Washington in his first presidential
proclamation, October 3, 1789

Thanksgiving is celebrated in America as a traditional holiday that has its roots in the Pilgrim harvest of 1620. Surprisingly, though, the United States of America is not the only country or culture to celebrate Thanksgiving. Harvest feasts or feasts of Thanksgiving have been celebrated for generations, from the ancient Greeks to modern-day Canadians.

Well before there was established religion there was belief in spirits and a spirit life, both good and evil. Many ancient farmers believed that the crops they grew, everything from corn to wheat, had a spirit, in much the same way people today believe they have a spirit. The farmers feared that cutting the crops would release the spirit, which would then seek revenge on the farmer.

Harvest festivals of that time, festivals we now call Thanksgiving in the United States, were to celebrate conquering those spirits.

In today's world, fewer people rely on a bountiful harvest to get through the winter. After all, it's pretty rare that you can't just go to the supermarket to pick up an apple or can of corn. These days however Thanksgiving is still a celebration of life and the bountiful harvest we have in every way.

Canada

Celebrated on the second Monday in October, observance of a Canadian Thanksgiving officially began in 1879, but like the American Thanksgiving, it has its roots in hundreds of years of European traditions. Generally, however, most Canadians will agree that while an Englishman named Martin Frobisher had a great deal of influence on today's Thanksgiving, the holiday is really based in the traditions of many different events.

It is said that Canadian Thanksgiving was actually derived from a combination of three different events in history. The first began with the immigration of European farmers to Canada. While still living in Europe, it was traditional for farmers to hold harvest celebrations as a way of giving thanks for the good fortune of a successful harvest and an abundance of food. As part of the festivities, the farmers would fill a curved goat's horn with fruits and grains. Today Americans and Canadians alike still use this goat's horn, or as we now call it, cornucopia or horn of good plenty.

Around 1578, English navigator Martin Frobisher initiated what is probably the second event that has woven its way into current Canadian Thanksgiving traditions. Frobisher was an explorer who had been trying to find a northern passage that would take him to the Orient. While he did not succeed in his quest, he did establish a settlement in northern America, the province we now know as Newfoundland, and he did celebrate a harvest feast to give thanks for surviving his journey there. Later, other settlers followed in Frobisher's footsteps and continued his Thanksgiving ceremonies. Frobisher was later knighted, and an inlet of the Atlantic Ocean in northern Canada was named after him—Frobisher Bay.

The third event to define Canadian Thanksgiving ironically had a great deal to do with Canada's neighbor to the south, the United States. In 1621, the Pilgrims celebrated their first successful harvest in the New World, and in the 1750s this celebration was brought to Nova Scotia by American settlers. During the American Revolution, there were a great deal of Americans who considered themselves Loyalists, remaining faithful to English government. When the Revolutionary War broke out, many of these Loyalists moved to Canada, bringing along the American tradition of Thanksgiving.

In 1879, the Canadian Parliament officially declared November 6 a national holiday and a day of Thanksgiving. Over the years however, the date changed several times until on January 31, 1957, Parliament proclaimed that the "2nd Monday in October be a Day of General Thanksgiving to Almighty God for the bountiful harvest with which Canada has been blessed." One of the reasons Canadian Thanksgiving is celebrated so much earlier than American Thanksgiving is simply that Canada is farther north and has an earlier harvest time than its neighbor to the south.

Maybe not so surprisingly, a traditional Canadian Thanksgiving often includes many of the same foods that can be found on an American Thanksgiving table—home-baked bread, apple pie, cranberry sauce, roasted turkey, fresh vegetables, mashed potatoes, squash, and stuffing.

August Moon Festival—Chinese Thanksgiving

Chung Ch'ui or the August Moon Festival is one of most celebrated Chinese holidays. Starting with the ancient Chinese and continuing on today, the festival falls on the fifteenth day of the eighth lunar month. The festival is not only a celebration and way to give thanks for a bountiful harvest, but Chung Ch'ui is considered the birthday of the moon. In honor of this special day the Chinese make "moon cakes," round, yellow cakes that resemble the moon. As a way to say thank you, friends and relatives send moon cakes to one another.

In addition to the celebration of the moon and giving thanks for a good harvest, Chung Ch'ui is also meant to give thanks for freedom. Legend says that there was a time when China was being systematically conquered by many different armies, invaders who were quickly taking over Chinese homes and land. Homeless and starving, the Chinese felt as if there was little they could do to protect themselves, until an organization of civilians came up with a plan.

In order to get the message across to all Chinese people that it was time to stand together and fight their invaders, Chinese women baked moon cakes and distributed them to every family in the village. Inside each cake they had baked a secret message regarding the time when they would gather together and stand against their enemies.

Thanks to those very special moon cakes, and very brave women, China's invaders were overthrown and easily defeated. A special day that the Chinese still happily celebrate now.

Besides moon cakes, Chinese families celebrate their Thanksgiving with a meal of roasted pig and harvested fruits. Tradition says that during the three-day festival flowers fall from the moon and those who see them will be rewarded with good fortune.

Min Festivals—Egyptian Thanksgiving

Thanksgiving for the Ancient Egyptians was a celebration in honor of Min, the god of fertility and Chief of the Heavens. In addition, Min was seen as a rain god or someone who promoted the fertility of nature and especially the growing of grain.

Unlike many other festivals, the Min Festivals were usually held in the spring. Instead of a thanksgiving for a bountiful harvest, the Egyptians celebrated the beginning of planting season. The celebration usually included the Pharaoh as he joined in a parade and presided over the celebratory feast. Much like Thanksgiving in the United States, the Egyptians included music, dancing, and sports into their celebration.

Thesmophoria—Greek Thanksgiving

Celebrated in the lunar month Pyanopsion, Thanksgiving in Ancient Greece was a celebration in honor of Demeter, the goddess of grain. Although Pyanopsion has no meaning to us now, it was probably around October. While little is known about the actual events that took place during this festival, historians have discovered some of the practices or celebrations the Greeks probably took part in.

It is thought that the harvest centers around Demeter's morning over the abduction of her daughter Persephone by Hades during which time she refused to eat or feed the world until the conflict was resolved. Once Persephone was returned, Demeter rejoiced by giving the gift of agriculture to mankind.

In honor of this and to ask Demeter to give them a bountiful harvest, married Greek women would set out for three days of celebration. On the first day, the ascent or Anodos, the women would set up camp in the hillside sanctuary of Demeter Themophoros, sleeping in two-person leafy shelters.

The second day of the festival was called Nesteria or the fast. On this day the women fasted and insulted one another. This is thought to be an imitation of Demeter during the loss of her daughter.

The third and final day of the festival was called Kalligeneia or Fair Offspring and was spent giving offerings to Demeter in honor of the torchlight search for Persephone. During the final night of the festival the women descended from the hill in a torchlight ceremony.

Sukkoth—Hebrew Thanksgiving

The 3,000-year-old Jewish harvest festival of Sukkoth begins on the fifteenth day of the Hebrew month Tishri (usually September or October) and continues for seven days. Much like the Chinese harvest festival, Sukkoth is more than just a celebra-

tion of thanksgiving for a bountiful harvest. Sukkoth is a celebration to honor the protection God gave the Israelites during
the years spent wandering the desert after their exodus from
Egypt.

Known by different names—*Hag ha Succot*, the Feast of the
Tabernacles and *Hag ha Asif*, the Feast of Ingathering—Sukkoth
gets its name from the huts (succot) that Moses and the Israelites were forced to live in during their wanderings. Since the
group needed to be mobile, succots were made of branches and
leaves and were easy to assemble and disassemble and easy to
carry.

In honor of Sukkoth and these Israelites, Jews today build
their own succot and decorate them with fruit and flowers in
the four days between the end of Yom Kippur and the beginning
of Succoth. During the eight days of Succoth many families will
sleep in their shelter, although in colder climates most only eat
meals there.

Niiname-sai—Japanese Thanksgiving

While many of today's harvest or thanksgiving traditions go
back hundreds and even thousands of years, the festival in
Japan is still very new. It wasn't until 1948 that Japanese officials declared a national day of thanksgiving or a celebration
for a bountiful harvest. It was at this time that November 23rd
was designated as the day to honor labor by paying respect to
workers, celebrate the year's harvest, and show mutual ap-
preciation for one another.

The harvest ceremony called Niiname-sai in Japan is one of
great celebration and thanks. It is during this time that the Em-
peror dedicates the year's rice harvest to the gods and tastes it
for the first time at the Imperial Household.

Thanksgiving Resources

Books

Thanksgiving 101: Celebrate America's Favorite Holiday With America's Thanksgiving Expert, by Rick Rodgers (Broadway Books).

One hundred of the best Thanksgiving recipes by one of America's most popular cooking teachers. Not only do you get the recipes that Rick Rodgers has collected through years of teaching his Thanksgiving cooking classes, but you get menus, trade secrets, advice on shopping, and even tips for vegetarians.

Holidays: Recipes, Gifts and Decorations: Thanksgiving & Christmas, by Martha Stewart (Random House).

Nobody does it quite like Martha with her decorating and menu tips.

Season's Greetings: Cooking and Entertaining for Thanksgiving, Christmas, and New Year's, by Marlene Sorosky and Geoffrey Nilsen (Chronicle).

A great source for cooking and party ideas.

Thanksgiving Cookery, by James W. Baker, Elizabeth Brabb, and Lisa Adams (Brick Tower).

James Baker, director of research at Plimouth Plantation, captures the essence of our country as he explores the development and evolution of the Thanksgiving holiday through recipes.

Thanksgiving: Festive Recipes for the Holiday Table (Williams-Sonoma Kitchen Library), by Chuck Williams, Kristine Kidd, and Allan Rosenberg (Time-Life).

This Thanksgiving find everything you need for a delicious holiday gathering in one book.

Web Sites

Annie's Home Page:
http://www.annieshomepage.com/thanksgivinghistory.html
  The history of Thanksgiving.

Aristotle's Thanksgiving:
http://home.aristotle.net/thanksgiving
  Facts and trivia about Thanksgiving.

Bountiful Thanksgiving:
http://www.kate.net/holidays/thanksgiving
  One of the best sites with plenty to do for kids and adults including history, recipes, crafts, games, and trivia.

Food Network:
http://www.foodtv.com/holidays/thanksgivingturkeyguide
  Tips on all your holiday cooking.

National Turkey Federation:
http://www.turkeyfed.org
  Tips on cooking your turkey.

Not Just for Kids Thanksgiving:
http://www.night.net/thanksgiving
  History, recipes, facts, and crafts.

Plymouth, Massachusetts, Homepage:
http://pilgrims.net/plymouth
  History and facts.

Thanksgiving on the Net:
http://www.holidays.net/thanksgiving
  History, facts, and recipes.

Thanksgiving Recipes:
http://www.thanksgivingrecipe.com/default.asp
  Recipes.

Thanksgiving:
http://www.2020tech.com/thanks
  History and recipes.

Thanksgiving:
http://deil.lang.uiuc.edu/web.pages/Holidays/Thanksgiving.html
Facts, recipes, quizzes, games, and fun.

Thanksgiving Entertainment

Thanksgiving Stories for Children

The Thanksgiving Story, by Alice Dalgliesh and Helen Sewell (Aladdin).
The story of the *Mayflower* voyage to the New World, the settlement at Plymouth, and the first Thanksgiving.

A Visit to Grandma's, by Nancy Carlson (Viking).
Thanksgiving offers an unexpected twist with a visit to Grandma, who has relocated to a Florida condo. Meeting the family in her new red sports car, Grandma whisks them all out of their old familiar traditions and into her new world, a world of fish and chips and store-bought pies.

Cranberry Thanksgiving, by Wende Devlin (Aladdin).
When someone steals Grandmother's famous recipe for cranberry bread, Grandmother is furious. Luckily the thief included the delicious recipe in the book. A great activity book for children.

Molly's Pilgrim, by Barbara Cohen (Beech Tree Books).
Molly's classmates tease her about being different, making her wish she and her family could move back to New York or Russia. When students make fun of the Pilgrim doll Molly's mother makes, simply because it looks like a Russian peasant, Molly's teacher explains that Pilgrims still come to America to find freedom from persecution.

Squanto's Journey, by Joseph Bruchac and Greg Shed (Silver Whistle).
Children will be fascinated by this lesser-known perspective on the Thanksgiving tradition.

The Hoboken Chicken Emergency, by Jill Pinkwater and Daniel Manus Pinkwater (Aladdin).
Instead of bringing home the family's Thanksgiving turkey, Arthur returns with Henrietta—a 266-pound chicken with a mind of her own.

Thanksgiving at the Tappletons', by Eileen Spinelli, Maryann Cocca-Leffler, and Judith Stuller Hannant (HarperCollins).

Nothing seems to go right at the Tappletons' Thanksgiving this year, and it is up to Grandma to remind everyone that there's more to Thanksgiving than a turkey and trimmings.

How Many Days to America?, by Eve Bunting (Clarion).

The story of a Caribbean family forced to flee from their homeland for the freedom of America. When they find what they are looking for, their prayers and hopes are celebrated by offering thanks as the Pilgrims did.

Three Young Pilgrims, by Cheryl Harness (Bradbury Press).

A story based on the Allerton family's experiences between 1620 and 1621.

Oh, What a Thanksgiving!, by S. Kroll (Scholastic).

A little boy looks at how the preparation of the Thanksgiving feast today differs from the original feast of the Pilgrims and Indians.

If You Sailed on the Mayflower in 1620, by Ann McGovern (Scholastic).

A great book of answers to those questions children ask about the Pilgrims and the *Mayflower* voyage.

The Pilgrims' First Thanksgiving, by Ann McGovern (Scholastic).

A historically accurate account of how the children the Plymouth Colony helped make the first Thanksgiving possible.

Samuel Eaton's Day: A Day in the Life of a Pilgrim Boy, by Kate Waters (Scholastic).

A story that follows Samuel (a Pilgrim) through work and play in an early American settlement in 1627.

Sarah Morton's Day: A Day in the Life of a Pilgrim Girl, by Kate Waters (Scholastic).

A story that follows Sarah (a Pilgrim) through work and play in an early American settlement in 1627.

Movies and Videos

A Charlie Brown Thanksgiving
This heartwarming tale first appeared in 1973 and has entertained generations of Peanuts lovers ever since.

Pocahontas
The Disney cartoon about the brave and free-spirited Pocahontas who defies her tribe to pursue her true love, John Smith.

Rugrats—Thanksgiving
Kids will love watching the very popular Rugrats and the Thanksgiving festivities at the Pickles house.

The Waltons: A Thanksgiving Story
When it comes to holidays, nobody does it like the Waltons in this favorite, which will be sure to charm the entire family.
And for the older folks. . . .

The Accidental Tourist
When armchair traveler Macon Leary, devasted by the death of his son, meets the kooky and aggressive Muriel Pritchett, his life starts to change in unimaginable ways.

Annie Hall
The Oscar-winning Woody Allen classic. A must-see.

Dances with Wolves
Another wonderful film. This Oscar-winning classic film about a Civil War soldier who befriends a Sioux tribe and eventually becomes one of them, is a wonderful addition to any Thanksgiving weekend.

The Daytrippers
When suburban wife Eliza stumbles upon a love letter the day after Thanksgiving that she thinks is intended for her husband, she turns to her family for advice. They all pile into the family station wagon on a road trip to Manhattan to track the husband down. A funny, touching comedy.

Little Big Man
The wonderful film about Jack Crabb, the 121-year-old man who reminisces about his life as a pioneer, adopted Indian, friend of Wild

Bill Hickok and survivor of Custer's Last Stand. A terrific movie about the treatment of Native Americans.

Plymouth Adventure

Oscar winner for special effects, this Spencer Tracy film tells the story of the Mayflower captain who sailed the settlers from England to New England in the seventeenth century.

Music

Thanksgiving: A Windham Hill Collection, by various artists.

Thanksgiving, by Creek Bend.

The Great Thanksgiving, by Joseph Franz Wagner, Don Gillis, and Reginald De Koven.

APPENDIX B

Thanksgiving Timeline

Early Times to Pre-U.S. Revolution Traditions

Before the arrival of the Pilgrims, American Indians had many of their own traditions of giving thanks, especially the Seneca Indian liturgy of thanksgiving (which can be found in Chapter 2).

1621

This is the year most famous for the first Pilgrim feast held near Plymouth, Massachusetts, in celebration of the Pilgrims' first success-ful harvest. This is the feast usually referred to as the First Thanksgiv-ing and the feast talked about in Chapter 1. Since this feast was never repeated, or made an annual event, it can't officially be considered the start of the Thanksgiving tradition that we know today. In fact, since the Pilgrims were devoutly religious, they didn't even call this first event a feast of Thanksgiving. To them Thanksgiving was not a time to eat, but a time to pray and fast. Nevertheless, the 1621 feast has become a model for the Thanksgiving celebration in the United States.

1630

Recorded as the year of the first Thanksgiving in the Massachu-setts Bay Colony, this feast was celebrated to honor the voyage of John Winthrop's ships from England. Because the passage was diffi-cult and stormy, Governor Winthrop declared a day of Thanksgiving for the ships' safe arrival. Governor Winthrop said, "We kept a daye of thanksgiving in all the plantations."

1775

A full year before the signing of the Declaration of Independence, a proclamation of prayer was written to ask that the entire North American continent set aside a day of prayer and fasting. The procla-mation had an amazing impact, uniting the American people in spirit.

1776

Before George Washington was given the daunting task of becoming this country's first president, he was a leader in more ways than one. On the day set forth by Congress as a day of Thanksgiving, George Washington and his troops, moving close to Valley Forge, deliberately stopped, despite the open fields they were in and the bitter weather they were facing, to celebrate the first Thanksgiving. As one early surgeon so eloquently said, "Mankind is never truly thankful for the benefits of life, until they have experienced the want of them."

Two hundred years later, the National Thanksgiving Commission was instituted in the George Washington Chapel at Valley Forge.

1795

George Washington gives the first Thanksgiving proclamation.

1863

It wasn't until our country was faced with Civil War that people again begin to consider the importance of a national day of prayer and Thanksgiving. In 1863 Abraham Lincoln declared, "We have been recipients of the choicest bounties of Heaven . . . we have grown in numbers, wealth and power as no other nation has ever grown, but we have forgotten God."

During some of the most tragic years our country has ever faced, Lincoln restored the neglected presidential proclamations. Since Lincoln's speech, every president has issued a Thanksgiving proclamation.

1926

Macy's Department Store sponsored the first Macy's Thanksgiving Day Parade. Since balloons weren't introduced until 1927, this first parade consisted of employees in costume, floats, bands, and live animals borrowed from the Central Park Zoo.

1975

In honor of the two hundredth anniversary of a National Day of Prayer and Thanksgiving, President Gerald R. Ford was presented with the book *America Prays Together*, the first collection containing two hundred years of National Prayer and Thanksgiving Proclamations.

Thanksgiving Charities

If you want to help but don't know how, take a look at this list of charities. When you have so much to be thankful for, it is nice to help those who don't.

Action Against Hunger, USA
875 Avenue of the Americas, Suite 1905
New York, NY 10001
http://www.aah-usa.org
    International humanitarian relief network that focuses on eradicating famine and malnutrition worldwide.

America's Second Harvest
35 East Wacker, Suite 2000
Chicago, IL 60601–2200
http://www.secondharvest.org
    The nation's largest hunger-relief organization, with a national network of more than two hundred food banks and food-rescue programs.

American Jewish World Service, Inc.
45 West 36th Street, 10th Floor
New York, NY 10018
    A nonsectarian organization founded to help alleviate human suffering, poverty, hunger, and disease and respond to human and natural disasters throughout the world.

The American Red Cross
PO Box 37243
Washington, DC 20013
http://www.redcross.org
    The American Red Cross is a humanitarian organization that exists to help people prevent, prepare for and respond to emergencies and to provide relief for the victims of disasters.

Children's Hunger Relief Fund
182 Farmer Ln., Suite 200
Santa Rosa, CA 95405
http://www.chrf.org

An international Christian organization that provides emergency relief in the form of food, clothing, medical care, shelter and education.

CityCares
1605 Peachtree Street, Suite 100
Atlanta, GA 30309
http://citycares.org/national/default.asp?

A national organization that helps people get involved on a local level with projects that include feeding the hungry, tutoring children, working with the elderly and homeless, improving the environment, and a host of other activities.

Citymeals-on-Wheels USA
355 Lexington Avenue
New York, NY 10017
http://www.citymeals.org/html/cmow_usa.html

Citymeals-on-Wheels delivers meals to homebound seniors on weekends, holidays, and in times of emergency.

God's Love We Deliver
166 Avenue of the Americas
New York, NY 10013
http://www.godslovewedeliver.org

This New York–based organization consists of volunteers who cook and deliver meals to people living with AIDS.

Habitat for Humanity
Partner Service Center
Habitat for Humanity International
121 Habitat St.
Americus, GA 31709
http://www.habitat.org

Founded in 1976, this international housing organization builds affordable housing for low-income families worldwide.

Heifer Project International, Inc.
1015 Louisiana Street
Little Rock, AR 72202
http://www.heifer.org
   A nonprofit organization that works to alleviate hunger, poverty, and environmental degradation.

The Hunger Project
15 East 26th Street, #1401
New York, NY 10010
http://www.thp.org
   The Hunger Project empowers people to achieve self-reliant progress in health, education, nutrition, and the status of women.

Institute for Food and Development Policy, Inc.
398 60th Street
Oakland, CA 94618
http://www.foodfirst.org
   Value-based solutions to hunger and poverty. Institute for Food and Development Policy, Inc., organizes for the right of all people to feed themselves.

Make-a-Wish Foundation
http://www.wish.org
   An organization that grants the wishes of children with life-threatening illnesses.

Manna International Relief and Development
PO Box 3507
Redwood City, CA 94064
http://www.nohunger.org
   Provides agricultural development and health and educational assistance in the United States and around the world.

Native American Rights Fund (NARF)
http://www.narf.org
   A non-profit organization that provides legal representation and technical assistance to Indian tribes, organizations and individuals nationwide.

Ronald McDonald House
http://www.rmhc.com

An organization working to better the lives of children and their families around the world by creating, finding, and supporting programs that directly improve the health and well-being of children.

Salvation Army
http://www.salvationarmyusa.org

Perhaps best known for their bell-ringing troops deployed to local malls during the holiday season, the Salvation Army runs charitable programs all over the world, including thousands of food distribution centers and soup kitchens.

Thanksgiving Memory Album

If you haven't already, start a Thanksgiving Memory album. Use the space provided in this book, or buy a separate book just for the occasion. Each year take a moment to photograph everyone together, either around the table or piled on the couch. Then record names and a few thoughts or special memories from that day. It won't be long before the album becomes the first thing the grandchildren go for each year, looking to see how much everyone has grown or to share the special stories from Thanksgiving past.

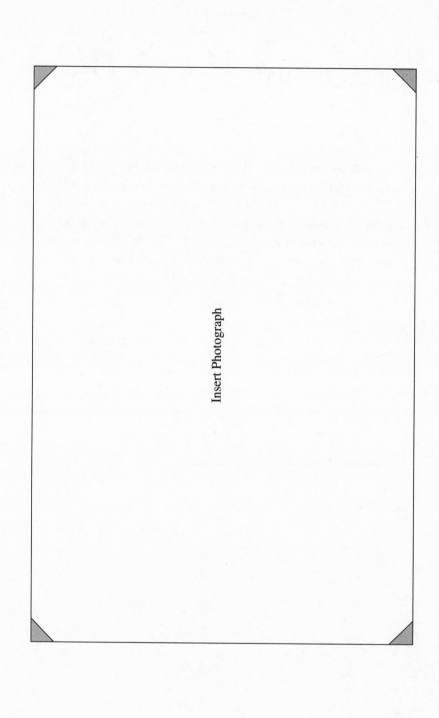

Insert Photograph

Date ——————

Names of
Guests ————————————————————

Special
Memories ———————————————————

Insert Photograph

Date ————

Names of
Guests ————

Special
Memories ————

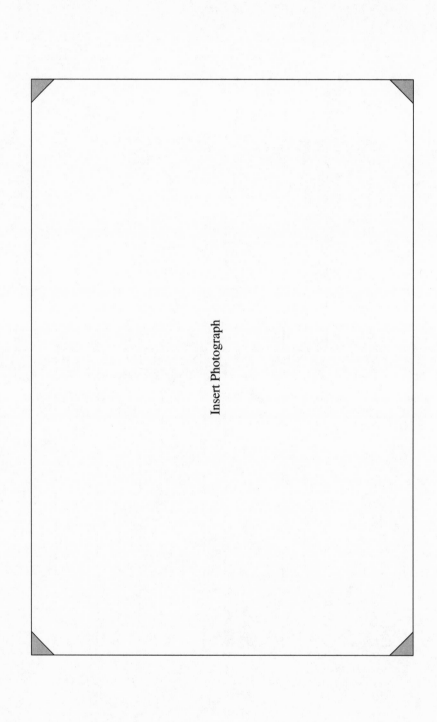

Insert Photograph

Date ————

Names of ————
Guests

Special ————
Memories

Index